Motivating Children and Young Adults to Read 2

Edited by James L. Thomas
and Ruth M. Loring

ORYX PRESS
1983

The rare Arabian Oryx is believed to have inspired the myth of the unicorn. This desert antelope became virtually extinct in the early 1960s. At that time several groups of international conservationists arranged to have 9 animals sent to the Phoenix Zoo to be the nucleus of a captive breeding herd. Today the Oryx population is over 400 and herds have been returned to reserves in Israel, Jordan, and Oman.

Library of Congress Cataloging in Publication Data
Main entry under title:

Motivating children and young adults to read—2.

  Bibliography: p.
  Includes index.
    1. Children—Books and reading—Addresses, essays, lectures.   2. Youth—Books and reading—Addresses, essays, lectures.   3. Young adults—Books and reading—Addresses, essays, lectures.   4. Reading—Addresses, essays, lectures.   I. Thomas, James L., 1945–
II. Loring, Ruth M.
Z1037.A1M9   1983   028.5'5   82-42924
  ISBN 0-89774-046-7

For Helen Overstreet
who has dedicated her life to motivating
young people to find ''the best'' in themselves.

Contents

Preface

The motivational factors that stimulate a person to want to participate in the reading process from early childhood through the young adult years remain an area of interest and investigation for both practitioners and researchers. How to determine, capture, and then maintain the interest of individuals in the reading process are the subjects addressed in volume two of *Motivating Children and Young Adults to Read*.

As a result of the positive responses received from teachers, librarians, and reading specialists to the first volume by the same title, the editors have, over the past three years, continued to read the literature relating to motivational techniques and programs that have proven to be successful with children and young adults. The same selection criteria used in volume one have been applied in judging suitable articles for this volume. As a result:

- each article is current (published after 1978);
- each is written in a readable format by an author who is experienced in the area;
- each presents practicable ideas;
- each presents content based on learning theory; and
- each discusses techniques which have proven to be successful.

The contributors' section of this book serves to verify the credentials of those chosen for inclusion.

Each of the essays has been placed in one of four major sections, entitled: "Attitudes and Interests," "Methodology," "Programs," and "Activities." The first section dealing with attitudes and interests includes assessment techniques for discovering individual factors which stimulate the desire to read. Methodology addresses the means to motivation from both theoretical and practical perspectives. Overall strategies for organizing, implementing, and evaluating reading programs are presented in the third section. Finally, articles relating to individual and/or group activities offering specific suggestions for motivating students to read are presented in the fourth section. Although such placement has been made according to the special area being addressed, it should not be assumed that each section is mutually exclusive. The volume concludes with a selective, annotated bibliography of materials for additional reference.

Ruth M. Loring
James L. Thomas

Contributors

J. Estill Alexander, Ed.D., is Professor and Coordinator of Reading and Language Arts, University of Tennessee, Knoxville, TN. "A Scale for Assessing Attitudes toward Reading in Secondary Schools" by J. Estill Alexander and Regina Tullock-Rhody is reprinted with permission from the authors and the International Reading Association. It originally appeared in *Journal of Reading* (April 1980, pp. 609–14).

Larry M. Arnoldsen is Assistant Professor, Department of Secondary Education and Foundations, College of Education, Brigham Young University, Provo, UT. "Reading Made Necessary, Naturally" is reprinted from *Journal of Reading* (March 1982, pp. 538–42) with permission from the author and the International Reading Association.

Michael J. Ash is Professor, Department of Educational Psychology, Texas A & M University, College Station, TX. The article "Motivating Students to Actively Engage in Reading," by William H. Rupley, Michael J. Ash, and Timothy R. Blair appeared in *Reading Psychology: An International Quarterly* (volume 3, #2, pp. 143–48). It is reprinted with permission from the authors and the publisher. Copyright © 1982 by Hemisphere Publishing Corporation, New York, NY.

Timothy R. Blair is Associate Professor in Reading Education, College of Education, Department of Educational Curriculum and Instruction, Texas A & M University, College Station, TX. "Motivating Students to Actively Engage in Reading" by William H. Rupley, Michael J. Ash, and Timothy R. Blair appeared in *Reading Psychology: An International Quarterly* (volume 3, #2, pp. 143–48). It is reprinted with permission from the authors and publisher. Copyright © 1982 by Hemisphere Publishing Corporation, New York, NY.

Carolyn R. Burch is the Chapter I Reading Coordinator for Charles Maclay Junior High School, Los Angeles City Unified School District. She is also a part-time instructor at California State University, Northridge, CA. "Management Systems in Secondary Reading Classrooms" first appeared in *Reading Horizons* (Spring 1980, pp. 207–14). It is reprinted by permission of authors Christine C. Smith, Carolyn Burch, Grace Warren, and the publisher. Copyright © 1980 by Reading Horizons, Western Michigan University, Kalamazoo, MI.

Betty M. Collins is Elementary Consultant, Ohio Department of Education, Division of Elementary and Secondary Education, Columbus, OH. Sandra McCormick and Betty M. Collins coauthored the article "A Potpourri of Game-Making Ideas for the Reading Teacher" which originally appeared in *Reading Teacher* (March 1981, pp. 692–96). It is used with permission from the authors and the International Reading Association.

Marilyn A. Colvin, Ed.D., is Director of Reading Education, Houston Baptist University, Houston, TX. "A Recreational Reading Program for Disabled Readers: It Works!" by Marilyn A. Colvin and Elton Stetson is reprinted from *Reading Horizons* (Summer 1980, pp. 247–51). Reprinted by permission of the authors and the publisher. Copyright © 1980 by Reading Horizons, Western Michigan University, Kalamazoo, MI.

Clyde G. Colwell is Assistant Professor of Reading Education, Department of Curriculum and Instruction, Kansas State University, Manhattan, KS. "Humor as a Motivational and Remedial Technique" originally appeared in *Journal of Reading* (March 1981, pp. 484–86). Used with permission from the author and the International Reading Association.

Bonnie Cramond is a resource teacher in the Lafayette, Louisiana Gifted Program. She is also on staff at the University of Southwestern Louisiana, Lafayette, LA. "Developing Creativity through the Reading Program" by Charles Martin, Bonnie Cramond, and Tammy Safter is reprinted from *Reading Teacher* (February 1982, pp. 568–72) with permission from the authors and the International Reading Association.

Nicholas P. Criscuolo is Supervisor of Reading, New Haven Public Schools, New Haven, CT. "Reading Motivation through the Teacher-Parent Partnership" originally appeared in *Momentum* (December 1980, pp. 21–23). This article is reprinted with permission from the author and *Momentum*, Journal of the National Catholic Educational Association, Washington, DC. "Rx for Your Kids: 28 Great Games to Improve Reading Comprehension" is from *Instructor* (October 1980, pp. 88–90). It is reprinted with permission from the author and the publisher. Copyright © by The Instructor Publication, Inc.

Mary Jane Gray is Associate Professor and Chairperson, Department of Curriculum and Instruction, Loyola University of Chicago, IL. "Bringing Children and Books Together" appeared in *Reading Horizons* (Summer 1979, pp. 292–97). It is reprinted by permission from the author and the publisher. Copyright © 1979 by Reading Horizons, Western Michigan University, Kalamazoo, MI.

John T. Guthrie writes the "Research Views Column" for *Reading Teacher*. "Reading Interests" is reprinted with permission from the author and the International Reading Association. It originally appeared in *Reading Teacher* (May 1981, pp. 984–86) and is an ERIC document in the public domain.

Hilary Taylor Holbrook is Research Assistant, ERIC Clearinghouse on Reading and Communication Skills, National Council of Teachers of English, Urbana, IL. The ERIC/RCS report "Motivating Reluctant Readers: A Gentle Push," originally appeared in *Language Arts* (April 1982, pp. 385–89). Copyright © 1982 by the National Council of Teachers of English. Reprinted by permission of the publisher and the author.

Dan Jackson is a teacher at Spotswood High School, Spotswood, NJ. He is also a freelance writer, with articles appearing in *Phi Delta Kappan, Commonwealth, National Catholic Reporter*, and *The New York*

Times. His article, "Books in the Bronx: A Personal Look at How Literature Shapes Our Lives," was first printed in *Media and Methods* (March 1980, pp. 14–17, 44). It is reprinted with permission of the author and *Media and Methods* magazine, a publication of the American Society of Educators. Copyright © 1980, North American Publishing Company, Philadelphia, PA.

Deborah R. Jansson, coauthoring with Theresa A. Schillereff, wrote the article "Reinforcing Remedial Readers through Art Activities." It first appeared in *Reading Teacher* (February 1980, pp. 548–51) and is used with permission from the International Reading Association.

Norma B. Kahn is the author of "Helping More Students Become Mature Readers," which first appeared in *English Journal* (March 1980, pp. 51–53). Copyright © 1980 by the National Council of Teachers of English. Reprinted by permission of the publisher and author.

Ruth J. Kurth is Associate Professor of Reading Education, College of Education, North Texas State University, Denton. Her introduction was written for this volume.

John Lewis is Professor of Psychology, Winona State University, Winona, MN. "A Reading Attitude Inventory for Elementary School Pupils" originally appeared in *Educational and Psychological Measurement* (Summer 1979, pp. 511–13). It is reprinted with permission from the author and publisher.

Sandra McCormick is Assistant Professor, Faculty for Exceptional Children, Ohio State University, Columbus, OH. "A Potpourri of Game-Making Ideas for the Reading Teacher" by Sandra McCormick and Betty M. Collins originally appeared in *Reading Teacher* (March 1981, pp. 692–96). It is used by permission of the authors and the International Reading Association.

Charles Martin is Assistant Professor, Department of Curriculum and Instruction, University of Southwestern Louisiana, Lafayette, LA. "Developing Creativity through the Reading Program" by Charles Martin, Bonnie Cramond, and Tammy Safter originally appeared in *Reading Teacher* (February 1982, pp. 568–72). It is reprinted with permission from the authors and the publisher, the International Reading Association.

Corlea S. Plowman was formerly Public Information Coordinator for Schools, Newport News, VA. "Tell Your Story with a Reading Fair" by Concetta Wilson-Gebhardt and Corlea S. Plowman originally appeared in *Reading Teacher* (February 1980, pp. 555–58). It is reprinted with permission from Corlea S. Plowman, Edward W. Carr (Public Information Coordinator, Newport News Public Schools, Newport News, VA), and the International Reading Association.

Elana Rabban is director of Library Media-Audiovisual Services for the Scarsdale School District, Scarsdale, NY. "Reaching the Able but Unwilling Reader" is reprinted from *School Library Journal* (December 1980, p. 37) with permission from the author and publisher. Copyright © 1980 by R. R. Bowker Company/ A Xerox Corporation.

"Reading" is reprinted by special permission of *Learning,* The Magazine for Creative Teaching, December 1980. Copyright © 1980 by Pitman Learning, Inc.

William H. Rupley is Associate Professor and Coordinator of the Reading Program, Department of Educational Curriculum and Instruction, Texas A & M University, College Station, TX. "Motivating Students to Actively Engage in Reading" by William H. Rupley, Michael J. Ash, and Timothy R. Blair is reprinted from *Reading Psychology: An International Quarterly* (volume 3, #2, pp. 143–48) with permission from the authors and the publisher. Copyright © 1982 Hemisphere Publishing Corporation, New York, NY.

Tammy Safter is an educational consultant, specializing in assessment and counseling in the area of gifted/creative education. She is also a part-time instructor at North Georgia College, Dahlonega, GA. "Developing Creativity through the Reading Program" by Charles Martin, Bonnie Cramond, and Tammy Safter originally appeared in *Reading Teacher* (February 1982, pp. 568–72). It is reprinted by permission of the authors and the International Reading Association.

Pat Scales is Media Specialist, Greenville Middle School, Greenville, SC. She is also an adjunct instructor at Furman University, Greenville, SC. "Parents and Students Communicate through Literature" which first appeared in *VOYA* (June 1981, pp. 9–11) is reprinted with permission from the author and VOYA. Copyright © June 1981 Voice of Youth Advocates, P.O. Box 6569, University, AL.

Theresa A. Schillereff wrote the article "Reinforcing Remedial Readers through Art Activities" with Deborah R. Jansson. It appeared originally in *Reading Teacher* (February 1980, pp. 548–51). Used with permission from the International Reading Association.

Naomi K. Skriloff is Reading Consultant for Hallen School, Mamaroneck, NY. She is involved in diagnostic services, pre- and posttesting, diagnostic/prescriptive instruction, remedial and corrective instruction, supervision of tutorial services, and resource services to the staff. "RBIs: Reading/Baseball Ideas" appeared in *Teacher* (April 1980, pp. 64–65). It is reprinted with permission from the author.

Christine C. Smith is Professor, California State University, Northridge, CA. She is the director of Secondary Education and teaches English and reading. "Management Systems in Secondary Reading Classrooms" by Christine C. Smith, Carolyn Burch, and Grace Warren is reprinted by permission of the authors and the publisher. It originally appeared in *Reading Horizons* (Spring 1980, pp. 207–14). Copyright © 1980 by Reading Horizons, Western Michigan University, Kalamazoo, MI.

Lewis B. Smith is Professor of Elementary Education, College of Education, University of Idaho, Moscow, ID. "Sixth Graders Write about Reading Literature" originally appeared in *Language Arts* (April 1982, pp. 357–63). It is reprinted with permission from the author and publisher. Copyright © 1982 by the National Council of Teachers of English.

Elton G. Stetson, Ed.D., is Associate Professor, Department of Curriculum and Instruction, University of Houston, Houston, TX. "A Recreational Reading Program for Disabled Readers: It Works!" by Marilyn A. Colvin and Elton Stetson was first printed in *Reading Horizons* (Summer 1980, pp. 247–51). It is reprinted with permission from the authors and the publisher. Copyright © 1980 by Reading Horizons, Western Michigan University, Kalamazoo, MI.

William H. Teale is Assistant Professor, Division of Education, The University of Texas at San Antonio. "Assessing Attitudes toward Reading: Why and How" is reprinted with permission from *Australian Journal of Reading* (June 1980, pp. 86–94). Used with permission from the author and the Australian Reading Association.

Regina Tullock-Rhody is a teacher with the Knoxville, TN county school system. She coauthored with J. Estill Alexander "A Scale for Assessing Attitudes toward Reading in Secondary Schools" which originally appeared in *Journal of Reading* (April 1980, pp. 609–14). It is reprinted with permission from the authors and the International Reading Association.

Grace A. Warren is an English and reading teacher at Charles Maclay Junior High School, Los Angeles City Unified School District, Los Angeles, CA. She is also the English department chairperson at the school. "Management Systems in Secondary Reading Classrooms" by Christine C. Smith, Carolyn Burch, and Grace Warren was originally printed in *Reading Horizons* (Spring 1980, pp. 207–14). It is reprinted with permission from the authors and the publisher. Copyright © 1980 by Reading Horizons, Western Michigan University, Kalamazoo, MI.

Lea-Ruth C. Wilkens is Associate Professor, University of Houston at Clear Lake City, Houston, TX. Her teaching responsibilities include children's literature, and in particular, topics such as "Modern Trends in Children and Young Adult Literature," "Methods of Teaching Reading in the Elementary School," and "Selection of Library Materials." She is completing a book for the American Library Association presenting the media specialist's perspective of learning how to read. Her article "The School Library—The Alpha and Omega of Your Elementary School Reading Program" appeared in *Reading Horizons* (Fall 1979, pp. 55–59). It is reprinted with permission from the author and the publisher. Copyright © 1979 by *Reading Horizons*, Western Michigan University, Kalamazoo, MI.

Concetta Wilson-Gebhardt died approximately two years ago. She was Director of Reading and supervised the entire reading program for the Newport News Public Schools, Newport News, VA. Her article "Tell Your Story with a Reading Fair," coauthored with Corlea S. Plowman, is reprinted with permission from Edward W. Carr (Public Information Coordinator, Newport News Public Schools, Newport News, VA), Corlea S. Plowman, and the International Reading Association. It first appeared in *Reading Teacher* (February 1980, pp. 555–58).

Introduction

A functioning democracy requires that its members be literate. Therefore, one of the goals of public education in a democracy must be the development of students who are proficient in reading and writing. The current emphasis on accountability in American education is evidence that the American people value the skills of reading and writing and recognize that they are essential to a continuing democracy.

But literacy proficiency is not a stable plateau that once reached is retained for life, for like any skill which is not used frequently, literacy will degenerate from neglect. Thus, it is not enough that students merely master the essential skills of reading and writing; in order to maintain these skills throughout their lifetimes, they must be practiced and fostered daily. True accountability in education, therefore, mandates the development of students who not only can read, but who are willing to read widely because they value reading as a positive and worthwhile process.

Helping students develop into able, eager, and avid readers is a continuing process which depends upon many factors for success. "The desire to read is a resultant of a present need, the push of the past, and the pull of the future" (Strang, 1969). Thus, the climate in which reading instruction takes place becomes one of the most influential factors for developing motivated readers. The instructional climate which will enhance motivation for reading needs to foster: (1) a sense of success, (2) a sense of acceptance and self-worth, and (3) a sense of enthusiasm for learning.

A sense of success is crucial to the development of students who value reading and pursue independent reading tasks. The perception that students have about their competence to succeed at tasks is a potent motivating factor. Success in a task almost always begets future successes. Students who have come to look upon their experiences with the printed page as a series of successful encounters are more apt to return to print over and over again. The teacher and/or librarian who has learned to provide a curriculum which promotes continued reading success can contribute much to students' development of lifelong reading habits. Individuals who encourage successful experiences with print will provide many opportunities for growth in small, manageable steps and will make certain that students recognize and value their own successes. A climate of success also needs to have ample amounts of time set aside for meaningful practice, for no skill is ever honed to perfection without continuous practice in a relatively risk-free environment.

A positive instructional climate also needs to foster students' self-acceptance as well as success. There is considerable research evidence which indicates that students' concepts of themselves play an important role in their motivation for reading. The educator who values students for who they are, rather than for how well they perform, is demonstrating to all students that they do indeed have intrinsic worth as individuals. People's perceptions of themselves are influenced to a great extent by the attitudes of those around them. The instructor's attitude of acceptance can influence both the students' perceptions of themselves as well as their perceptions of each other. If one is secure about his/her individual worth, s/he can afford to try difficult tasks without undue fear of failure or rejection because of failure. A teacher demonstrates acceptance of students by noticing individual students, by actively listening to them, and by paying particular attention when they express their feelings. The person, not the reading skill, needs to be the focal point of a reading program that fosters lifetime reading habits (Otto/Smith, 1970). Often, in the rush to manage all of the intricacies of daily life in the classroom, the needs of students become secondary. By being aware of students' present problems and hopes for the future, the teacher and/or librarian can communicate that students are valued members of the school community.

Finally, an educator who encourages the development of intrinsic motivation for reading will be filled with a sense of enthusiasm for the results of reading. The powerful impact such an individual can have as a reading model cannot be overstressed. When students perceive that the teacher views reading as a significant and valued activity, they develop the understanding that reading has relevance and value even in a world which is bombarded with nonprint media. The individual who becomes excited because of new knowledge can help students experience the excitement that learning new knowledge through print can generate. In his discussion of the mature reader, Gray (1959) states that s/he has many compelling reasons for reading. If a teacher values the student in the reading program, s/he will recognize students' interests and will use these interests to build units of study based on these topics. A consuming desire to learn something about a particular topic of interest has sent many a reluctant reader to the library. The educator who delights in students' discoveries through reading communicates an important message about the value of reading.

The focus of this book of readings is the development of an educational climate for reading which is based on success, self-acceptance, and enthusiasm for reading. In this collection, the editors have chosen articles which are current, are written by experts in the field, and contain theoretically valid ideas and techniques for motivation. It is their intent that these articles will assist teachers and librarians in providing a climate which will foster the development of mature, motivated readers.

Ruth J. Kurth

REFERENCES

Gray, William S. "The Nature of Mature Reading." *The School Review* 62 (October 1959): 394.

Otto, W., and Smith, R. J. *Administering the School Reading Program.* Boston: Allyn and Bacon, Inc., 1970.

Strang, R. "The Reading Process and its Ramifications." In *Elementary Reading Instruction,* Beery, A.; Barrett, T.; and Powell, W. R., Eds. Boston: Allyn and Bacon, Inc., 1969, p. 12.

Section I
Attitudes and Interests

Assessing Attitudes toward Reading: Why and How

by William H. Teale

Effective assessment of a student's reading is marked by several characteristics. Its purpose is to lead directly to improvement in the student's reading. It is in accord with a sound theory of the social-psychological-linguistic process known as reading. It focuses not only upon reading *per se* but integrates also information about the student's writing, speaking and listening in order to develop an overall picture of strategies and abilities in reading. It is continuous and interwoven with teaching; that is to say, assessment is a daily part of classroom interaction with the student, not a special undertaking conducted two or three or whatever number of times per year. Furthermore, careful assessment attends also to the affective dimensions of reading.

THE IMPORTANCE OF STUDENTS' ATTITUDES TOWARD READING

There are two general reasons why attitude merits attention in the assessment of reading. In the first place, it is widely accepted that a positive attitude toward reading is important for achievement in reading. Even though to date there is relatively little empirical evidence to support such a contention, few practitioners or researchers would deny that attitude plays a central part in becoming literate.

The second sense in which reading attitude is important relates not to achievement but to the characteristics of a reader. Huck (1973, p. 305) discusses this point directly when she says:

> If we teach a child to read, yet develop not the taste for reading, all of our teaching is for naught. We shall have produced a nation of ''illiterate literates''—those who know how to read but do not read.

One characteristic of individuals who do choose to read is their positive attitude toward reading. Without such an attitude the most that can be expected is a person who is a *won't reader,* Huck's *illiterate literate.* Thus, if a goal of schools is to develop students who both can and want to read (and I think it is), educators need to pay special attention to the extent to which the *taste for reading* is being fostered.

It is evident that a strong case can be made for the need to focus on reading attitude in teaching and in assessment. In fact, within the last few years many authors have addressed this issue, arguing that the affective factors in reading need emphasising as much as the cognitive ones (see, for example, Alexander and Heathington, 1975 and Johnson, 1979). The importance of reading attitudes and the need to make assessment of them integral to the teaching process are ideas which are being recognised increasingly. However, before putting any reading attitude assessment program into operation, before focusing upon the *how* of such an endeavour, teachers and other school personnel must have a good understanding of what it is that's to be measured.

WHAT IS ATTITUDE TOWARD READING?

At first glance it would appear that consensus has been reached on the answer to this question. There is general agreement that a person's attitude toward reading is the *disposition to respond in a favourable or unfavourable manner to reading* (after Oskamp, 1977). However, *disposition* is a term which can be and has been interpreted in a number of ways in the measurement of reading attitude. For example, Estes et al.

(1976) and Alexander and Heathington (1975) have both defined attitude toward reading in terms similar to those just put forth. Yet, when one examines the scale which each author has developed to measure the reading attitudes of students in grades four through six, it becomes clear that the two have operationalised the concept of attitude toward reading differently.

One feature of Heathington's scale is that it provides the opportunity for the teacher to assess *areas of a child's reading environment toward which he (the child) may feel positively or negatively* (In Alexander and Filler, 1976, p. 27). That is to say, the scale is devised so that the child's answers indicate how she feels about reading in various physical/organisational settings (free reading in the classroom, organised reading in the classroom, reading at the library). It can be inferred from this provision that Heathington believes that *aspects of a child's reading environment* are important considerations when assessing reading attitude. Estes et al., on the other hand, make no provision of this type for interpreting the results from their scale, and they include only one item which could be said to measure directly any of these *environmental aspects* of reading attitude. Another dissimilarity between the two scales can be seen in the degree to which each is designed to measure the child's enjoyment of reading: the Estes scale devotes five of fourteen items to this purpose; Heathington, only two of twenty-four.

Additional differences between the scales could also be cited. The point, however, is that even though on the general level these authors employ the same definition of reading attitude and thus would appear to be in accord with each other, content analyses of the scales themselves reveal conceptually nontrivial differences in the way in which *disposition* has been operationalised. Moreover, differences of this kind are found not only in the comparison between the Estes and Heathington scales; such incongruities are the rule rather than the exception among instruments which purport to be measuring individuals' general dispositions toward reading.

To complicate matters even further, some researchers have shunned the *disposition* definition, arguing that measures based upon such a notion are at best vague. These researchers have elected instead to specify as precisely as possible what it is they are attempting to assess. However, the specifications of different researchers vary.

Overall, then, there exist a number of possible definitions of attitude toward reading, ranging from the *disposition* approaches to various theoretically specific conceptualisations. The task for educators, of course, is to settle upon one definition so that appropriate assessment can be conducted. That being the case, the question which arises is, *which of the possible interpretations is the most sound*. Unfortunately I have no answer for this question (nor I suspect does anyone else); there simply is not *a* best account of what reading attitude is. The most that can be said is that, in the world of education, what is meant by attitude toward reading *depends*. It depends upon the objectives of the teacher and the school. It depends upon the needs of the community which the school serves. It depends upon the reasons why the assessment is being performed.

HOW CAN ATTITUDE TOWARD READING BE ASSESSED?

Attitudes are mental constructs. They cannot be seen and cannot be measured directly. Behaviours are the only clues we have to the attitudes which students hold. It is from reading and reading-related activities and from what people say about reading that we can infer their attitudes. There are three general methods for collecting information that can help in making these inferences: observation, self-report instruments and projective techniques.

Observation

Observation should play a key role in any attempt to assess students' attitudes toward reading. It is a most useful technique because it can be conducted over an extended period of time and in an unobtrusive manner, thus maximising the probability that you have seen the pattern of the students' typical behaviours. These characteristics make observation potentially the most ecologically valid way in which you can obtain information about reading attitudes.

However, observation as an assessment procedure is not without inadequacies. It can be a hit or miss, highly subjective, largely uninformative (or even misleading) endeavour if not utilised in the proper manner and to its fullest extent. Unlike an *objective* reading attitude scale, the value of observation is highly dependent upon the skill of the person conducting it. Thus, the teachers must be familiar with the principles of sound observational technique. There is not space here to detail the particulars of conducting and interpreting observations in the classroom. Strang (1969) gives a good overview of the procedures, and Alexander and Filler (1976) make practical suggestions for using observation to assess reading attitudes. In addition Healy (1965) and Rowell (1972) have developed observational checklists of behaviours which reflect reading attitude.

Observation is potentially the greatest strength of the reading attitude assessment program. Teachers, using their skill in observation combined with knowledge of their students, can actualise that potential.

Self-Report Instruments

On a self-report instrument the student directly provides responses which indicate her attitude toward reading. Self-report is most often the type of measure used in the formal assessment of reading attitude. The instrument itself may be a standard interview, a questionnaire, an activity preference technique or a reading attitude scale of some sort. The measures discussed in the preceding section of this article are all of the self-report type. Many other reading attitude self-report instruments have been developed over the years, and the reader is referred to Alexander and Filler (1976) and Summers (1977) for reviews of them.

A self-report measure can serve as a quite useful device for assessing reading attitude—if it has proved satisfactory in two respects. On the one hand the scale or questionnaire must be adequately constructed and validated. A second requirement is that the measure in question must be capable of evaluating reading attitude *as reading attitude has been defined for purposes of the assessment.* The importance of assuring that an instrument is based upon a conception of reading attitude which coincides with the conception adopted by the assessor(s) has been discussed at some length above and will not be repeated here. Suffice to say that unless this condition is met, even the statistically best reading attitude instrument in the world won't tell you what you want to know.

By satisfying these two criteria, then, you will learn as much about students' attitudes toward reading as a self-report instrument can tell. This does not mean, though, that any self-report device provides the whole story. There are limits to what such a measure can reveal. Also there is a problem inherent in the use of self-report: students tend to tell teachers what they think teachers want to hear. Thus, they may give what in the school situation are more socially acceptable responses denoting a positive attitude toward reading when, in fact, their attitudes are not so positive. This difficulty can be overcome to some extent by scale construction techniques (disguising the purpose of the instrument) and by administration procedures (assuring students

that there are no right or wrong answers, that their responses will not be graded, and so on). However, such provisions should not be the only means relied upon to ensure that what the student says on a self-report scale is a true reflection of his reading attitude. The results from self-report can be corroborated by findings from observation and projective techniques. This triangulation process, or multimeasure approach, is a procedure which will be discussed further after we examine projective techniques.

Projective Techniques

Projective techniques are so named because it is assumed that respondents will project their feelings and beliefs onto the stimulus to which they are asked to respond. Typically subjects are presented with a simple picture, a word or incomplete sentence, the task for them being to interpret what is seen, provide an associated word or complete the sentence. It is believed that individuals will perceive the stimulus in terms of their own needs and dispositions, thus revealing their beliefs and feeling in the interpretations they provide. For instance, a student might be shown a picture of individuals engaged in reading or reading-related behaviours. The student would be asked to describe the scene and characteristics and behaviours of the person(s) in the picture. These unstructured responses would then be analysed to determine the student's attitude toward reading.

Projective instruments provide a theoretically interesting way of assessing reading attitude. They hold special promise for measuring the reading attitudes of young children: the response format for them is much more natural than that of self-report, and the stimulus need not be so verbally oriented. Also with projective measures there is less tendency for students to provide socially desirable answers, simply because the purpose of the instrument can be readily disguised. Of course, projective measures are subject to certain practical problems. They necessitate special training on the part of the person employing them for there is a great deal of skill required to administer the device and interpret the results. This factor must be kept in mind when deciding upon actual assessment techniques.

WHICH METHOD TO USE?

Observation, self-report instruments and projective techniques, then, are the three general methods by which information about students' reading attitudes may be gathered. The question which now arises is, *which method(s) should you employ in your assessment program?* Remember that the assessment of attitude poses a special problem. Attitude toward reading cannot be measured directly; it can only be inferred. Naturally you want to ensure that your inference about Elizabeth's reading attitude is an accurate one. The best way to do so is to adopt a multiple indicator, or multi-measure, approach. As the name suggests, the multi-measure approach uses data gathered from more than one source in drawing inferences about students' attitudes. This method maximises the probability that the inferences you have drawn are valid ones. A judgment based on a single or limited source of information is quite often inaccurate: a student may be less than truthful on a self-report instrument; the fact that Warren has not read a book in the first six weeks of school may be due to unusual personal or home circumstances rather than a reflection of a negative attitude toward reading. In other words, you need to analyse findings from observation with those from self-report and projective instruments, allowing each to be interpreted in light of the other so that a picture of a student's reading attitude emerges. The multi-measure approach can help you ensure an accurate assessment because each judgment can be cross-checked and validated by various types of information.

Thus, each of the techniques described can be used to good advantage in your reading assessment program. Observation should form the heart of your evaluations. In addition to naturalistic observation in which students' reading and reading-related behaviours are studied in different contexts, the observational checklists of Healy (1965) and Rowell (1972) may prove useful. I would recommend also the use of one self-report instrument. Such a measure would be relatively easy to administer, score and interpret and will provide helpful information. Depending upon the thoroughness of your observations, these two techniques may be sufficient for arriving at valid inferences about students' attitudes toward reading. Of course, projective technqiues can also be used to supply additional data where needed.

This is the *how* I suggest for assessing reading attitude. Notice that no recommendations have been made as to which self-report instrument should be utilised or what in particular should be looked for in observation. Such recommendations cannot be made simply because the specifics of reading attitude assessment should be governed by the definition of attitude toward reading which is adopted, and as argued above, the selection of that definition depends.

Readers may feel that these recommendations for means of assessing reading attitude in the classroom are rather vague. However, I do believe that as you become more familiar with the diverse ways of conceptualising attitude toward reading, the particulars of the appropriate procedures will become apparent.

CONCLUSION

Attitudes need to be taken into account in the teaching and assessment of reading. This means that each teacher should pay special attention to evaluating the reading attitudes of her students. In conducting that evaluation, the teacher should adopt a definition of attitude toward reading that is both theoretically sound and suited to his classroom-school-community circumstances. Observation, self-report and projective techniques are all useful means of gathering information about students' attitudes. As with any assessment program, the assessment of reading attitude should not be an end in itself but a means of improving the teaching and learning of reading. Seen in this manner reading attitude assessment can make a positive contribution to the reading education of all children.

REFERENCES

Alexander, J. E. and Filler, R. C. *Attitudes and Reading.* Newark, Delaware: International Reading Association, 1976.

Alexander, J. E. and Heathington, B. A crucial fourth component in reading instruction-attitudes. *Tennessee Education.* 5, 32–36, 1975.

Estes, T. H., Roettger, D. M. and Johnstone, J. P. *Estes Attitude Scales: Elementary Form.* Charlottesville, Virginia: Virginia Research Associates, 1976.

Healy, A. K. Effects of changing children's attitudes toward reading. *Elementary English.* 42, 269–72, 1965.

Huck, C. S. Strategies for improving interest and appreciation in literature. In A. Beery, et al. (Eds.) *Elementary Reading Instruction: Selected Materials* (2nd ed.). Boston: Allyn and Bacon, 1973.

Johnson, B. Assessing reading attitudes: What can teachers do? Paper presented at the Fifth Australian Reading Conference, Perth, August 1979.

Oskamp, S. *Attitudes and Opinions.* Englewood Cliffs, New Jersey: Prentice-Hall, 1977.

Rowell, C. G. An attitude scale for reading. *The Reading Teacher.* 25, 442–47, 1972.

Strang, R. *Diagnostic Teaching of Reading* (2nd ed.). New York: McGraw Hill, 1969.

Summers, E. G. Instruments for assessing reading attitudes: A review of research and bibliography. *Journal of Reading Behavior,* 9, 137–66, 1977.

A Reading Attitude Inventory for Elementary School Pupils

by John Lewis

The purpose of this paper was to describe the results of an effort to develop a reading attitude scale that would yield reliable and valid scores for third, fourth, and fifth-grade pupils. The Estes Reading Attitude Scale (Estes, 1971) was seen as a desirable model even though trials had shown that it was not reliable for elementary school pupils.

PROCEDURE

It was thus decided to develop the attitude scale by making major revisions of the Estes. First, many items were changed by reducing the level of reading comprehension needed for reliable responses. Second, the number of response categories was reduced from a Likert-type five-point scale to a three-point "Yes," "No," and "Sometimes" scale.

In the scoring plan, "Sometimes" was given a value 1 for all 20 items. Since items 1, 8, 11, 12, 16, and 17 were stated negatively, "No" was scored 2 with a "Yes" scored as 0. For the remaining 14 items, "Yes" was scored 2 points with "No" scored as 0.

PSYCHOMETRIC CHARACTERISTICS

Reliability

This new scale was administered to 214 third, fourth, and fifth-grade pupils enrolled in two elementary schools in rural southern Minnesota. Means, standard deviations, and corrected split-half reliability coefficients are presented in Table 1.

Magnitudes of the standard deviations indicate that among these pupils this scale is sensitive to individual differences in attitude toward reading. The reliability coefficients of .75, .69, and .72 suggest an acceptable level of consistency or reliability among patterns of responses.

TABLE 1. Means, Standard Deviations, and Reliability Coefficients on the Reading Attitude at the Three Grade Levels

	$\overline{X}$	S	Rel.
Grade 3(N=45)	24.3	5.5	.75
Grade 4(N=93)	26.7	4.3	.69
Grade 5(N=76)	26.4	4.4	.72

Validity

The scale was administered to a second group of 151 third, fourth, and fifth-grade pupils at the beginning of the next school year. A correlation of .33 ($p < .01$) was found between scores on the scale and teachers' ratings of apparent enthusiasm for readings taken in February. The teachers rated the pupils as having "high interest," "middle interest," or "low interest." The results of a comparison on mean attitude scores for pupils classified into each of the three groups are shown in Table 2.

Third, fourth, and fifth-grade pupils who were rated as having high interest in reading in February had

TABLE 2. Comparison of Mean Reading Attitude Scores for Pupils Later Classified According to Interest in Reading

N	Interest Level		
	High (N=50)	Middle (N=90)	Low (N=11)
X	28.8	25.9	23.5
s	3.9	5.2	3.2

$F(2,148)=8.96\ p<.01.$

a mean attitude score of 28.8 in September with the middle interest group scoring an average of 25.9 and the low interest group attaining a mean of 23.5. The differences among these means yielded an *F* ratio of 8.96 which reached the .01 level of statistical significance.

REFERENCE

Estes, T. H. A Scale to measure attitudes toward reading. *Journal of Reading*, 1971, 15 (2), 135–38.

Reading Attitude Inventory for Low Level Reading Ability

To be read to students   YES   NO   SOMETIMES

1. The only reason I read is for learning.
2. It is a good idea to spend money to buy books and other things to read.
3. I can find out many things from books, magazines or newspapers.
4. Reading a book is fun for most people.
5. Reading is a good thing to do when I have some extra time.
6. Telling someone (the class) about a book I have read is a lot of fun.
7. I would rather read than play most games.
8. Reading is just for boys and girls who study all the time.
9. Books are usually interesting enough to read all the way to the end.
10. Reading is a lot of fun for me.
11. I get tired reading after a little while.
12. Most books or stories are too long.
13. Reading whatever I want to read teaches me many things.
14. I wish there was more time for me to read.
15. There are many books that I would like to read.
16. Books should be read only when I have to for school.
17. I would rather do something else besides read.
18. Some time should be used for reading during summer vacation.
19. I like to get books or other things to read for presents.
20. I like to read to other people.

                                                    SCORE

A Scale for Assessing Attitudes toward Reading in Secondary Schools

by Regina Tullock-Rhody and J. Estill Alexander

Since the way students feel about reading is closely involved with their reading achievement, teachers need to be aware of techniques that may be used to assess attitudes. This article talks about some common approaches, and describes the development of a paper and pencil instrument for use with secondary students which appears to be valid and reliable.

Structured teacher observation of relevant behaviors over time is one of the most valuable (if not the most valuable) ways to assess attitudes (Alexander and Filler 1976, p. 19). Time constraints may make this difficult for secondary teachers, however, since they see students for a short time each day and may teach large numbers of students each term.

What briefer techniques, then, are available? According to Smith, Smith and Mikulecky (1978, p. 84), it is possible to use paper and pencil tools, such as summated rating scales, to secure information about how students feel about reading. Such an instrument would provide valuable complementary data even if structured observation were planned, since a multimeasure approach adds meaning to the information available for classroom use (Zirkel and Greene 1976).

What are the requirements of an adequate paper and pencil device for classroom use? Heathington (1975, pp. 4–6) says such instruments should (a) require no reading on the part of the student, (b) be designed to be used early in the school year, (c) require minimal time for administration and scoring, (d) be reliable and valid, (e) take into account the fact that attitudes should be measured throughout the school experience, and (f) contain items truly representative of students' feelings toward reading.

A review of the available attitude measures for grades 7 to 12 revealed that none met all these require-ments adequately. The most frequent deficiency was that items on the instruments were not based on information about how the students themselves felt about reading. Only one instrument used information from students (Kennedy and Halinski 1975). In this scale items were generated from an open-ended questionnaire which, as will be noted later, may be limited by the students "first thoughts" or by her/his ability to communicate via a questionnaire. We agree with Oppenheim (1966, p. 32) that items should be gathered from a situation in which the information gained reflects the "richness and spontaneity of the situation." In general, an interview technique provides for greater richness and spontaneity than does a questionnaire.

Since no secondary school instrument was found that totally met the Heathington criteria noted earlier, we sought to devise an instrument that would meet these criteria.

DEVELOPING THE SCALE

The following procedures were used in the development of the secondary reading attitude scale: (a) selection of instrument type, (b) selection of population for gathering data, (c) pilot work, and (d) administration and readministration of the scale for validity and reliability checks.

Selection of Instrument Type

We considered several paper and pencil techniques, including the three most frequently used types—questionnaire, pairing techniques, and summated reading scales (Rhody 1978). The questionnaire was rejected because it often uses open-ended questions which permit students to give their "first" rather then their "best" responses and because it may discriminate against those students who have disabilities in reading, writing, or spelling. The pairing technique was rejected because it offers only two choices—reading and another activity. A student may like both to "read" and "play baseball," for example. However, "baseball" may be chosen because it has higher priority at the time of the response. The summated rating scale was considered a good choice because it permits students to express degrees of feeling about the behaviors or items sampled (i.e., strongly agree, agree, undecided, disagree, strongly disagree). Since degrees of feeling do indeed exist, we felt this paper and pencil technique was best for classroom use. Additionally, it could be designed to meet all the Heathington criteria.

The Populations

Seventh through twelfth graders from six urban schools and two rural schools in eastern Tennessee were used in various phases of designing the instrument. The students represented a wide range of socioeconomic and ability levels.

TABLE 1. Validity Data

Rating by Teachers	N	Mean Score	Standard Deviation	t
Positive	60	88.17	20.45	4.16*
Negative	60	74.45	15.05	

*$p < .001$

Pilot Work

The first phase of the pilot work consisted of individual interviews with 74 boys and 68 girls. A tape recorder was used to permit the interviewer (one of the authors) to concentrate on what the student was saying during the interview. Both Black (N=31) and White (N=111) students were interviewed.

The interviews were structured as follows. First, students were asked to describe the comments and behaviors of three people they know who like to read. Then students were asked to do the same for three people they know who do not like to read. The purpose of these two questions was to elicit possible statements for the attitude scale. Second, students were asked to describe a place they felt was conducive to reading. The

purpose of this question was to identify possible clusters of environments in which secondary students read.

Throughout this process, students were free to talk spontaneously and also to rethink their answers before proceeding to another part of the interview. During the questioning, the interviewer asked questions to elicit fuller responses.

From a synthesis of individual responses, the investigators were able to identify 33 discrete statements appropriate for use on the pilot scale. These statements were randomly ordered for a preliminary tryout.

The final phase of the pilot work involved administering the tryout scale to 204 students in grades 7–12. An item analysis was then performed to determine if all the items were discriminating between respondents with positive attitudes and those with negative attitudes. A correlation of 0.40 was determined to be acceptable for inclusion of an item on the final scale, since Downie and Heath (1970) suggest that ranges between 0.40 and 0.60 are acceptable for validity coefficients. Of the 33 items on the pilot scale, 25 correlated highly enough to be retained on the final scale.

Validity and Reliability

To provide data for validity and reliability, the revised instrument was administered to 349 students in two urban schools and two rural schools in eastern Tennessee.

Three indicants of validity for the scale are noted. First, the fact that the statements were constructed from comments made by secondary students themselves is viewed as an indicant of validity. The scale measures what selected secondary students think are important indicators. Second, 12 teachers were each asked to designate five of their students who they felt had the most positive attitudes toward reading and five of their students who they felt had the most negative attitudes toward reading. The results, shown in Table 1, indicate that the scale did discriminate between students perceived as having positive attitudes and those perceived as having negative attitudes. Third, the fact that the individual items retained on the final scale correlated at an acceptable level with the total scale is also seen as an indicant of validity.

The test-retest method was chosen to establish reliability since it measures temporal stability. An interval of one week was chosen as the test-retest period. According to Guilford and Fruchter (1973, p. 92), reliability coefficients should be "in the upper brackets of r values, usually 0.70 to 0.98." The results of the analysis of the data as computed by the SPSS program (Nie,

Rhody Secondary Reading Attitude Assessment

Directions: This is a test to tell how you feel about reading. The score will not affect your grade in any way. You read the statements silently as I read them aloud. Then put an X on the line under the letter or letters that represent how you feel about the statement.

SD-Strongly Disagree   D-Disagree   U-Undecided   A-Agree   SA-Strongly Agree

	SD	D	U	A	SA
1. You feel you have better things to do than read.	___	___	___	___	___
2. You seldom buy a book.	___	___	___	___	___
3. You are willing to tell people that you do not like to read.	___	___	___	___	___
4. You have a lot of books in your room at home.	___	___	___	___	___
5. You like to read a book whenever you have free time.	___	___	___	___	___
6. You get really excited about books you have read.	___	___	___	___	___
7. You love to read.	___	___	___	___	___
8. You like to read books by well-known authors.	___	___	___	___	___
9. You never check out a book from the library.	___	___	___	___	___
10. You like to stay at home and read.	___	___	___	___	___
11. You seldom read except when you have to do a book report.	___	___	___	___	___
12. You think reading is a waste of time.	___	___	___	___	___
13. You think reading is boring.	___	___	___	___	___
14. You think people are strange when they read a lot.	___	___	___	___	___
15. You like to read to escape from problems.	___	___	___	___	___
16. You make fun of people who read a lot.	___	___	___	___	___
17. You like to share books with your friends.	___	___	___	___	___
18. You would rather someone just tell you information so that you won't have to read to get it.	___	___	___	___	___
19. You hate reading.	___	___	___	___	___
20. You generally check out a book when you go to the library.	___	___	___	___	___
21. It takes you a long time to read a book.	___	___	___	___	___
22. You like to broaden your interests through reading.	___	___	___	___	___
23. You read a lot.	___	___	___	___	___
24. You like to improve your vocabulary so you can use more words.	___	___	___	___	___
25. You like to get books for gifts.	___	___	___	___	___

Scoring: To score the *Rhody Secondary Reading Attitude Assessment,* a very positive response receives a score of 5, and a very negative response receives a score of 1. On items 4, 5, 6, 7, 8, 10, 15, 18, 20, 22, 23, 24, and 25, a response of ''strongly agree'' indicates a very positive attitude and should receive a score of 5. On the remaining items, a ''strongly disagree'' response indicates a very positive attitude and should receive the 5 score. Therefore, on the positive item, ''strongly agree'' receives a 5, ''agree'' receives a 4, ''undecided'' receives a 3,'' ''disagree'' receives a 2, and ''strongly disagree'' receives a 1. The pattern is reversed on the negative items. The possible range of scores is 5×25 (125) to 1×25 (25).

Bent and Hull 1970) showed that the instrument falls within this range. The *r* obtained was 0.84.

SELECTED USES OF DATA

Data obtained from the administration of the scale have several uses. The authors recommend consideration of the following.

1. The scale may be used for pre and post assessments of change of attitudes in classrooms, schools, or school systems. Many funded programs require that some measure of feeling toward reading (or change of feeling toward reading) be included.

2. The scale may be useful in counseling individual students. Many secondary students have problems that stem at least partially from a poor attitude toward reading. This scale may help the teacher or counselor identify the student's feelings early in the school year. It should be noted that, in some instances, students may answer in ways that do not represent how they actually feel. If this is suspected, observation of relevant behaviors over time may be needed.

3. The scale may also be used to aid classroom teachers in understanding students' feelings toward areas of the reading environment. To assist teachers with this understanding, the statements on the scale have been grouped into clusters. The clusters were determined from student comments during the inteview situation and are as follows:

> School related reading: items 11, 18
> Reading in the library: items 9, 20
> Reading in the home: items 4, 10
> Other recreational reading: items 5, 17, 22, 24, 25
> General reading: items 1, 2, 3, 6, 7, 8, 12, 13, 14, 15, 16, 19, 21, 23

Data organized by clusters can aid the classroom teacher in creating more appropriate reading environments. For example, a teacher might compare a given student's attitude on the items concerning school related reading with the student's attitude toward other recreational reading. If the student indicated negative attitudes concerning school related reading yet positive attitudes toward other recreational reading, then the teacher might be able to adjust activities involving the school related reading portion of the program in ways that might be more appealing to the student.

REFERENCES

Alexander, J. Estill and Ronald C. Filler. *Attitudes and Reading*. Newark, Del.: International Reading Association, 1976.

Downie, N. M. and R. W. Heath. *Basic Statistical Methods*. New York, N.Y.: Harper & Row, 1970.

Frechtling, Joy. "Compensatory Reading Programs: A Discussion of Research Oriented toward Informing Federal Policy Makers." *Reading Research Quarterly*, vol. 13, no. 4 (1977–1978), pp. 473–81.

Guilford, J. P. and Benjamin Fruchter. *Fundamental Statistics in Psychology and Education*. New York, N.Y.: McGraw-Hill, 1973.

Heathington, Betty S. The Development of Scales to Measure Attitudes toward Reading. Unpublished doctoral dissertation, University of Tennessee, Knoxville, 1975.

Kennedy, Larry D. and Ronald S. Halinski. "Measuring Attitudes: An Extra Dimension." *Journal of Reading*. vol. 18, no. 7 (April 1975), pp. 518–22.

Nie, Norman H., Dale H. Bent and C. Hadlai Hull. *Statistical Package for the Social Sciences*. New York, N.Y.: McGraw-Hill, 1970.

Oppenheim, A. N. *Questionnaire Design and Attitude Measurement*. New York, N.Y.: Basic Books, 1969.

Rhody, Regina. The Development of a Reading Attitude Instrument for Grades Seven through Twelve. Unpublished doctoral dissertation, University of Tennessee, Knoxville, 1978.

Smith, Carl B., Sharon L. Smith and Larry Mikulecky. *Teaching Reading in Secondary School Content Subjects: A Bookthinking Process*. New York, N.Y.: Holt, Rinehart and Winston, 1978.

Zirkel, Perry A. and John F. Greene. "Measurement of Attitudes toward Reading in the Elementary Grades: A Review." *Reading World*, vol. 16, no. 2 (December 1976), pp. 104–13.

Reading Interests

by John T. Guthrie

Usually when we speak of a student's interests, we are referring to what he or she is attracted to. A person who is interested in a singer or a sport is thought to be attentive to it, to converse about it, to invest money in it, and in some cases to engross the Self in it.

Another meaning that attends the word *interest* is accomplishment. When we speak of a student who has a keen interest in marine life or archeology or banking or *Mad Magazine*, we communicate a measure of expertise. It is implied that the student has a higher than average knowledge or superior acumen in the object of interest. Although an interest often grips the person, the person treats the interest as a possession.

Teachers who engage children with reading materials are aware of the importance of interests. They know that learning requires sustained energy which, in turn, requires the use of materials that will attract and engross the students. High interest materials are intriguing, and students will study them with pleasure for a long period of time, whereas low interest materials are boring and do not command attention.

High interest materials are more fully comprehended than low interest materials. This has been a hunch or perhaps a cherished belief of many teachers. It is also supported by reasonably sound research. For example, Steven Asher reported that fifth grade children comprehended passages more fully if they indicated a high interest in the topic than if they indicated a low interest in it. The children's interests were measured with a technique in which children rated pictures on a scale from one to seven in terms of how much "you like it and would like to find out more about it." Comprehension was measured with a cloze task over passages clearly related to the topics of the pictures. Asher's findings occurred equally for both boys and girls and both White and Black children. Scores on the cloze tasks were approximately 30% higher for high interest than low interest materials for all groups. This study was reported in *Child Development* and is summarized in a chapter by Asher on "Topic Interest and Children's Reading Comprehension" in *Theoretical Issues in Reading Comprehension* by Spiro, Bruce, and Brewer.

The fact of high comprehension for high interest materials is not astonishing. The question of how to account for this finding is more problematic. A reflexive response, based on the first meaning of *interest*, is that high comprehension stems from increased attention to the content of the passage. For high interest materials children work harder to derive a large number of concepts, information, and inferences from the written material. Exactly how this increased effort or attention leads to improvements in comprehension is not stated in this account.

Another explanation for the finding that high interest materials are easily comprehended is based on superior background knowledge. In this case, it is assumed, and with some reason, that students know more about topics in which they are interested. Through attending to a topic by reading, listening, conversing, and watching television, students acquire information about it. This extended information base provides an advantage in comprehending passages on this particular topic.

The problem of whether the interest effect on comprehension is due to an attentional factor or higher background knowledge is not easy to solve. Several unsuccessful attempts are reported by Asher in his book chapter. A recent unpublished investigation sheds some light on this issue. In this study, the authors measured the interest of students on a variety of topics by asking them to rate how interested they were in pictures on these topics. The knowledge of students on topics for which they expressed very high or very low interest was measured with a separate test. Passages on these topics were constructed with the cloze procedure and given to the students to measure comprehension of passages on the topics. A standardized reading comprehension test was also administered for control purposes.

The findings were that after reading comprehension ability and interest were accounted for, knowledge contributed significantly to comprehension. Students with higher background information on the topics understood the passages more fully than students with less background. However, after accounting for reading comprehension and background knowledge, the level of interest did not influence comprehension significantly. In other words, when the students' knowledge about the topics was equated, their amount of interest did not increase or decrease their ability to comprehend passages on the topics.

These findings suggest that interest leads to knowledge which leads, in turn, to increased comprehension. Students who are interested in a particular topic are likely to have acquired information about it through a variety of in-school and out-of-school ac-tivities. Having this broader base of concepts, ideas, and facts enables them to comprehend passages on this topic more fully than students who do not have a similar knowledge base. Of course, students may often learn a great deal about a topic even though they have little interest in it. This relatively high knowledge base, even though it may be acquired and maintained reluctantly, will also produce a higher comprehension on passages of this topic.

Although one particular study is rarely conclusive, our best working idea must be that high interest materials are more easily comprehended than low interest materials by virtue of the knowledge this interest has generated.

The inclusion of high interest materials in a reading curriculum is advisable regardless of the outcome of this debate. However, the reason for the inclusion may be affected by it. High interest materials may serve as a means, a technique used by the teacher to attain a goal of higher comprehension. This view is supported by the attentional position. On the other hand, teachers may wish to include high interest materials simply because reading them represents the pursuit of individuality and self-actualization.

Bringing Children and Books Together*

by Mary Jane Gray

The author of good children's books devotes his talents to creating new worlds into which continuing generations eagerly seek entrance. How can a teacher help children to discover these new worlds? It has been said that in order to help children develop an interest in reading and a desire to read, the classroom teacher must be familiar with children's books. Much of the literature dealing with the teaching of reading seems to indicate that capitalizing on interests is a relatively recent practice, however, a glance back to the seventeenth century demonstrates that at least one individual would have been an ardent advocate of this procedure.

John Locke presented definite ideas on how children should be taught to read.

> When by these gentle ways he begins to be able to read, some easy, pleasant book should be put into his hands, wherein the entertainment he finds might draw him on (Meigs and Others, 1969, p. 54).

His comments sound remarkably similar to recommendations being made today.

> In all reading tuition the first aim should be to produce children and adults who want to read and who do read: the second aim should be to help them read effectively. If the second aim is given priority, it is probable that the first aim will never be achieved. In other words, neither recreational nor functional reading can be expected to be the end product of extended intensive instruction in reading skills. Reading must consist of recreational and functional activities from the very beginning (McKenzie in Williams, 1976, p. 53).

*"Bringing Children and Books Together" appeared in *Reading Horizons* (Summer 1979, pp. 292–97). It is reprinted by permission of the author and the publisher. Copyright © 1979 by *Reading Horizons*, Western Michigan University, Kalamazoo, MI.

Contrast these recommendations with Bettelheim's (1976) comments about the reading materials used to teach reading today. He believes that meaningful reading rarely enters the life of a child before third grade and by third grade the child's basic reading attitudes are fully established. He goes on to say our primers offer no meaning to children, and strongly urges that meaning be placed at the beginning of reading instruction, for this is the purpose of reading—to find meaning.

Is it possible to build a good reading program which capitalizes on children's interests? A firm, "Yes!" is the answer to this question. One way to capture their interest is by reading to the children as a part of the regular school day. An example from my elementary school teaching experience demonstrates the ease with which this may be accomplished.

A short period each day was devoted to reading to my second grade students. One of the authors most enjoyed by this class was Eleanor Estes. Several of *The Moffat* books were read to the group. Although these were children enrolled in a suburban school and about as far removed in actual setting and experience as they could be from the children in the stories, they could not wait for the chapter to be read each day. The feelings and activities of the Moffat children are universally found in each generation. This is one of the qualities which helps to ensure that a book will continue to be popular with children for years.

My own class of college student teachers has been required to spend a short period each day reading to their students. In one of these classes the student teacher found seven children who did not speak much English. The book she chose as the first one to read to the group was one of the *Frances* books by Russell Hoban. Only one little girl did not pay attention at first. By the middle of the story her interest had been piqued, and by the end she was up with the rest of the group at the teacher's end of the table looking over the top of the book to see what the teacher was reading.

In addition to acquainting the children with some of our literature, they also profited from these sessions in other ways including developing listening skills, increasing vocabulary, and becoming acquainted with various language patterns.

A second way to capture interest is to provide for children the opportunity to choose and read books in which they are interested. For this purpose the school library should provide picture books, story books, and informational books along with the opportunity for children to come frequently to the library to make their selections. The librarian can also play an important role by scheduling storytelling sessions for teachers and their classes.

The argument that the core of the reading program must be based on skill development is not a sound one. Huck supplies the best counter-argument.

> One of the best kept secrets in education is that children learn to read by reading. Most teachers overteach the skills of reading to the detriment of reading practice and enjoyment. Many primary teachers spend over half of their day teaching children how to read without ever giving them the opportunity for reading (1976, p. 600).

A second argument that there have not always been good books available can also be disproved by an examination of children's books, many of which were attainable early in our country's history. Just a few of the categories—adventure stories, humor and fantasy, family stories, historical fiction and history—provide ample evidence that there has always been something to appeal to each child's tastes.

ADVENTURE

One of the tales which was intended for adults, but which was enjoyed by children was *Pilgrim's Progress*. It is an allegory which describes the Christian soul on its journey to everlasting life, but children enjoy it as a good adventure story.

A second book written for adults, but once again enjoyed by children was Daniel Defoe's *Robinson Crusoe*. It, too, is an allegory, but the theme of it, man against nature, appeals to the adventurous spirit in all children. The story blended fact and fiction into an enticing tale that stimulates a child's imagination.

The third book which was written for adults and taken over by children was another adventure story,

Gulliver's Travels. It is an allegory which again combines adventure and suspense in a fictional setting. It is similar to *Robinson Crusoe* in that it deals with shipwreck and survival, but unlike *Robinson Crusoe* it deals with more than man's struggle with nature; it deals with man's struggle with man.

Howard Pyle's 1883 publication, *The Merry Adventures of Robin Hood of Great Renown, in Nottinghamshire,* continues in popularity at least partially because Pyle based his theme upon a struggle that all children understand, the struggle between good and evil. It contains some historical and geographical facts concerning medieval England, yet these are woven into a fabric of adventure and fiction which fascinates children.

Pyle expressed very well the impact that a good book has on young readers.

> In one's mature years, one forgets the books that one reads, but the stories of childhood leave an indelible impression, and their author always has a niche in the temple of memory from which the image is never cast out to be thrown into the rubbish-heap of things that are outgrown and outlived (Nesbitt in Meigs & Others), p. 287 from Abbot, C. *Howard Pyle: A Chronicle*. New York: Harper, 1925.

HUMOR AND FANTASY

In 1865 Lewis Carroll's *Alice's Adventures in Wonderland* appeared. This story was first told to children for their entertainment before it was written. It is a story of adventure filled with many improbable characters and situations. Perhaps it was one of the first stories with no other purpose than that of entertainment.

The Tale of Peter Rabbit developed out of a letter written to an ill child. The small size of the book and the very delicate and small illustrations done by Beatrix Potter are extremely well suited to children's taste. It seems strange when one considers the fact that this book has continued in popularity for seventy-five years that initially it had to be printed at the author's own expense.

Another book not favorably received at first was Kenneth Grahame's *The Wind in the Willows*. This book had its origin in bedtime stories Grahame told to his son of a water rat, a mole and a toad.

C. S. Lewis wrote the first of the Narnia series: *The Lion, the Witch, and the Wardrobe* in 1950. It was followed by six other books. From the first trip through the back of the wardrobe to the land of Narnia, children are held spellbound by Lewis's stories.

STORIES OF FAMILY LIFE

Henry Steele Commager wrote in the Introduction to *A Critical History of Children's Literature:*

> . . . Young Louisa Alcott, the spinster who never really understood children, and who wrote perhaps the greatest book to come out of the New World . . . Those little women of Concord have gone all over the world, they have gone into the hearts of children everywhere, giving them a feeling for America that nothing else gives in quite the same way.

Little Women is indeed an outstanding book. Alcott possessed the ability to make characters who live for the reader. She provided for children what they seem to want and need.

The *Little House Books* give to children a picture of life in an earlier time. Wilder's stories which contain an account of the life of the Ingalls family are very realistic. Although they were not written until the author's late middle age, they are very accurate. Details of life during those early times and in such a different setting from that familiar to today's children make these extremely appealing to young readers. Laura Ingalls Wilder, like Louisa May Alcott, was able to impart to children the feeling of love and security found in a strong family unit (Fisher, 1975).

HISTORICAL FICTION AND HISTORY

Allan Wheeler (1971) summed up very aptly the values of using trade books in the classroom.

> . . . Good trade books breathe life into people and places . . .
> Factual material will never be able to present the joys, sorrows, and problems of other times and people . . .
> The quality of writing and the beauty of the illustrations in good trade books will recreate the charm and lifestyle of other times and places. From such quality literature children can build a mental pool of experiences lost to them through purely factual reading materials.

Historical fiction is of great benefit in helping children to understand and appreciate history. It goes beyond the factual presentation found in textbooks and brings events and people to life for the reader.

Using information she had found for her biography of Paul Revere, Esther Forbes wrote *Johnny Tremain* which is very true to life. "It actually is a fictional study of the Boston Tea Party and the events leading up to it (Fisher, p. 162)."

Hendrick Van Loon's *The Story of Mankind* was the first Newbery winner. It, too, did more than present facts; it truly made history real for the reader.

Only a few of the very well known children's books have been included here. Even that small sample provides evidence that there have always been books which hold great appeal for children. The teacher's task is a two-fold one—to become acquainted with books for children and to see to it that children and these books are brought together as a regular part of the school day. To do this is to provide the key to the new worlds to be discovered in books and through such discovery reap the rewards to be derived from reading so well described by Sutherland and Arbuthnot.

> Books are no substitute for living, but they can add immeasurably to its richness. When life is absorbing, books can enhance our sense of its significance. When life is difficult, they can give a momentary relief from trouble, afford a new insight into our problems or those of others, or provide the rest and refreshment we need. Books have always been a source of information, comfort, and pleasure for people who know how to use them. This is as true for children as for adults (Sutherland & Arbuthnot, 1977, p. 4).

REFERENCES

Bettelheim, D. On learning to read. *The National Elementary Principal*. Sept.–Oct. 1976, 56, 6–14.

DePencier, I. *The History of the Laboratory Schools.* Chicago: Quadrangle Books, 1967.

Ellis, A. *A History of Children's Reading and Literature.* London: Pergamon Press, 1963.

Fisher, M. *Who's Who in Children's Books.* New York: Holt, Rinehart & Winston, 1975.

Gillespie, M. *Literature for Children: History and Trends.* Glenview, Illinois: Scott Foresman & Company, 1973.

Huck, C. *Children's Literature in the Elementary School* (3rd ed.). New York: Holt, Rinehart & Winston, 1976.

Huck, C. and D. Kuhn. *Children's Literature in the Elementary School* (2nd ed.). New York: Holt, Rinehart & Winston, 1968.

McKenzie, M. Schematic learning and reading in Williams, R. (ed.) *Insights into Why and How to Read.* Newark, Delaware: International Reading Association, 1976.

Meigs, C., A. Eaton, E. Nesbitt, and R. Viguers. *A Critical History of Children's Literature* (rev. ed.). New York: The Macmillan Company, 1969.

Smith, D. *Fifty Years of Children's Books.* Champaign, Illinois: International Reading Association, 1965.

Sutherland, Z. and M. H. Arbuthnot. *Children and Books* (5th ed.). Glenview, Illinois: Scott Foresman & Company, 1977.

Wheeler, A. Individualizing instruction in social studies through the use of children's literature. *The Social Studies.* 1971, 62, 162–170.

Books in the Bronx:
A Personal Look at How Literature Shapes Our Lives

by Dan Jackson

The crowd I grew up with in the Bronx during the 1960s had plenty of style and color, no geniuses as far as I know, and not much class. But quite a few of us had the cheek or the need to do things our own way. That's how we played. That's how we partied. And that's how we read books. John, for example, went wild with Catullus one year for no apparent reason. He would recite romantic or sexy lyrics halfway through our beer-blasts. Ten years down the line, he became probably the only IBM specialist whose first trip to Europe was highlighted by a visit to see the Catullus manuscripts in Venice. Fred liked Maugham. He read *The Moon & Sixpence, Of Human Bondage, Cakes and Ale,* and at least eight other works, while falling into and failing out of three high schools. And his vision of the world was shaped by those unrequired readings.

The girls were no different. Lorraine hated the three high schools she attended, but read enough detective fiction to compile a bibliography for a dissertation. Marian was bookish and bright. She even stayed in the same school for four years. None of us were ever surprised when she showed up at Orchard Beach with *Siddhartha, Pere Goriot* or *The Brothers Karamazov.*

Sweeper and Razz liked only sports stories, which they weren't allowed to read in school. Bill's teacher thought his passion for Jules Verne was ''just a stage.'' Ronny had a problem with his penchant for Sartre; what teacher would believe that a kid from the Bronx was really reading *Nausea* for the third time.

So, along with the streets, the crowds and the noise, along with the ghosts, flowers and animals that filled our walks in Poe Park, the Botanical Gardens and the Bronx Zoo, we all had this other thing in common:

our schools didn't recognize or exploit our enthusiasm for reading.

I was no exception. I failed English and Latin so often in my freshman and sophomore years that the director of guidance told me to forget about college. His intuition was supported by other givens: wrong neighborhood, wrong friends, wrong interests. I said nothing to him in response, even though I was embittered by the way he said I couldn't make it and hated him for saying it at all. So I went to work on 42nd Street for a year after high school, and then sneaked into college part time at night, like a cat burglar. Years later, at a conference where I was giving a paper on Socrates, I bumped into him. Yes, he was pleased that I was doing so well. No, he couldn't remember ever discouraging me in any way.

That only made the pain of his earlier judgment more pointed. But even back then, I knew deep down that he was wrong. Sure my grades stunk, but I understood everything Ronny and Bill told me about philosophy and science fiction. I could talk all day with Marian about plots and characters in novels. John said I'd really enjoy Latin if I ever got the chance to translate Catullus' dirty poems. Maybe they knew something about me that the school had missed.

In hindsight, of course, it's even possible to find a turning point. The impact of meeting my future wife, Lorraine, right after graduation changed me profoundly. Plato is right. No force educates the human spirit more beautifully than love.

People digest books in different ways. This is especially true of books that move us deeply. At a given time a certain student might be totally ready for anything from Plato's *Apology* to Segal's *Love Story*. How that book will be received, registered, and remembered depends more on the emotions of the reader than on the quality of the work or the number of people waiting in line to see the movie. No limited edition or deluxe binding or professorial pumping is going to make a book great for someone. Taking an entire class through the same story at the same time is like coralling tourists at one end of the Vatican Museum in order to herd them past centuries of art before lunch. It's economical. And senseless. In order for the magic to work, you must find your own way at your own pace.

During that year after high school I read what I wanted, and for the first time I liked what I read. Friends gave me books so I could write reports for them because I had more free time. I'd review plots to prepare them for the tests they had to take. I'd point out what I thought were the best passages, and share my enthusiasm. We started to find *our* stories, the ones we never tired of reading.

Because the food for thought we got in school was like the mush they served in the cafeteria, we began to hunt for writers the way gourmets look for restaurants. One year Joe read *Catch-22* six times. Ronny read everything by Sartre that was translated into English. John did Freud. I took Camus. We argued about them at parties for guys who were leaving for Nam. We sent paperbacks to APO numbers in San Francisco and waited for replies. We buried a friend who was killed in action. Then another. Then another. One day smoke from the South Bronx filled the air over the schoolyard where we hung out. We stopped playing and raced to the rooftop to watch. Billows of dark, stinking clouds erased the Manhattan skyline, the same skyline that had swelled our parents with hope when they emigrated from Ireland and Germany and Italy. But now the dream was burning. Camelot was in flames. Everything we learned in school meant less.

As the world of our childhood crumbled, we turned more and more to books for answers. We searched frantically for characters who had done what we hoped to do: survive . . . feel joy . . . find love. It was important to look in books for people who could do what was rarely done by the train conductors and cops who worked with our fathers. It was important to consider the countless stories that have bittersweet endings in order to learn whatever sorrow teaches, and to better appreciate the joy that seemed so elusive to us at that age. It was as important to do all this as it had been to make believe we were Yogi Berra or Whitey Ford or Mickey Mantle when, in earlier years, we played stickball outside Yankee Stadium.

That we read with such abandon was not unusual. Fanaticism flourished in our neighborhood. There were no doctors or lawyers or engineers living on Archer Street for us to use as role models. And many of our parents had fled European circumstances that generated extremism. We needed no teacher to tell us that ''Cosa Nostra'' and ''Sinn Fein'' were Italian and Gaelic expressions for ''our own law.'' It's true that two of us would eventually compete in the Olympics, another become a welterweight boxing champion, one play on a National League All-Star team and three enter the Peace Corps. But that only balanced the scale which sent others to Elmira, Sing Sing, and Attica.

I did not understand what compulsive or addictive reading meant then. Nor do I today. But I see many examples of it. Some kids read Tolkien religiously. Or Vonnegut. Or Hesse. At an earlier age they race through the Hardy Boys or Nancy Drew or James Bond; my five-year-old wants the same *Star Wars* primer read every night before he goes to sleep. This is not unique. Certain people in prisons or ghettos also read voraciously. I'm not sure exactly why—I suspect that escapism is part of the answer.

But I also think that many readers escape toward freedom, not away from reality, when they latch onto books that strike them personally. It may not be psychologically profitable for the mind to be constantly exposed to what oppresses the spirit, but it is fascinating to be one step removed from horrific experiences that parallel your own fears. This was known by writers long before the first disaster movie. It forced Lucretius, who believed that all life was a struggle in the dark, to depict the calm indifference of his shoreline philosopher who witnessed the drowning of those who would not be saved.

The freedom toward which fiction lets us flee is sometimes called Objectivity. Boys about to be drafted and girls who are pregnant don't always want to see eyewitness news coverage of battles and childbirth in living color. That's why they turn off upsetting television shows or close their eyes in movies. (Others gawk. People are different.) But those in pain need the possibility that fiction provides to consider the suffering of others from a distance. To leave your own country and culture and age, and explore the trauma of 19th century serfs or the anguish of 20th century Jews in *War and Peace* or *Babi Yar,* is to bridge even the gap between you and your supposed enemy. It is to be forced to admit, with Virgil, that there are tears everywhere and that human suffering touches our souls. Many kids in this country don't need Piri Thomas or Judy Blume to describe the mean streets and sterile suburbs they already know intimately, as much as they need Saint-Exupery and Dante to help them cope with spiritual vacuity.

To say that Ibsen or Sophocles or Yeats can help us understand the world more joyfully is to express faith in the ability of writers to do several things. It is to believe or imagine that they have fathomed their own human development so skillfully that they are able to find counterpoints everywhere in the experiences of others. So it is possible for a handsome young poet like T.S. Eliot to fully project a small part of his own adolescent loneliness into the jaded middle-aged manners of an imaginary J. Alfred Prufrock in order to write, at 20 years of age, the finest love poem of our time. This poetic magnification lets authors sense tragedy as well as joy with a fullness that others rarely know. But even in the sorrow of their characters, like Antigone or Yossarian, they seem to give their people a special ingredient—perhaps it's human frailty—which is to be celebrated, not regretted. And we enjoy the triumph of the author's tale by drying our eyes and passing the book on to someone else whose mind will also be uplifted by an acquaintance with such woe.

Whether they write about the sorrow of innocent suffering, or the brevity of love, or the outrage of injustice, authors everywhere reflect on human happiness. Their chief concern is how a good life can be described, concocted, destroyed, or sustained. And their chief ability is the vision that peers deftly into the souls of men and women who are faced, in youth or old age, with the absurd contradictions that beset life and suggest radical meaninglessness. That vision penetrates the pages of a great author's work and it lets readers see the sorrow and fear that fill the small victories of ordinary people. Characters may be shrill or brave or bumptious. They may be parodied, analyzed, or stereotyped. But they all present nothing more than mirrors for readers who can see either themselves or their neighbors—in stories not unlike their own.

The more widely one reads, the more obvious it becomes that there are greater similarities than differences between people, greater bonds than barriers between cultures, greater common denominators than divergencies between ages. Accepting the panoply of values and mores and aesthetics that is found in the literature of the world's nationalities enjoins us, as readers, not only to tolerate things outside our own experience, but also to bring into our world view a refreshing and liberating endorsement of the human family. It is to know and love what is perennially ours as children of the same fate. For none of us can read of the birth, bliss, and triumph of others without thinking of our own. None of us can reflect on sorrow or heartache without recalling what sadness we, also, have felt. None of us can read widely without showing the signs of having met many people in many places doing many things. To read more is to live more. And to live more means to understand the grace and power and joy of experience.

This clarity of perception is not the inevitable result of any professional encounter with a single discipline. I have known classics professors who were as pusillanimous and ugly as any punk I ever met on the street. The spirit that is opened in the way I have described belongs to anyone of any age or any ability who has found and fathomed the books that, for them, are really worth reading.

As we study older literatures, we search for the existential roots that relate us to all other people. We do this in the same way that we sift childhood memories. Try as we may, it is not possible to put all the parts of our puzzling stories into place. So we quite naturally depend on others, like grandparents or historical novelists, to fill in for us the disparate pieces of real or imagined knowledge that are missing because of local discontinuity or the imbecility of war. Through the attention it pays to writing, each generation perpetuates this exchange that assures the continuum of civilization's story. It is in no way surprising that the giants of modern thought—including bogeymen like Marx, Nietzsche, Kierkegaard, and Pound—began their apparently iconoclastic careers by first carefully reconstructing the past in programs of classical study. It was obvious to them, as it is obvious to others, that in order to know the present or predict the future, we must be familiar with the past. Anyone who reads widely admits the same, and acknowledges that to know one's self, it is first necessary to know the others from whom one descends and to whom one is drawn again in the completion of another of life's cycles.

We are each born with the same urge to gradually create our own sense of harmony. We each need to learn in our own way, and slowly. It used to be cute to say that, in order to teach Latin to Johnny, you had to know more about Johnny than about Latin. That's not cute, it's correct. To put students on the right reading tracks, schools might save the money they now dump into meaningless standardized tests, and follow these simple steps: (1) Ignore most of the data accumulated on the student. (2) Ask the student what he or she likes to read. (3) Match the book to the person. (4) Do not expect quick results.

The tensions and joys each young person feels focus on the hope of reaching somewhere a separate peace. It's a slow and difficult climb, not unlike scaling a treacherous peak, and must take place in stages. There are false starts and backslides, and times when long labor seems to produce little headway. But as the kids stretch out for yet a higher handhold, they can draw strength from the stories that speak to them of who has tried and who has failed, and who has tried again.

The man who taught me how to read left school in the second grade. Our painstaking lessons on the old piano bench each night after supper are among my fondest childhood memories. Learning to read with him meant learning the virtues of a good bus driver: patience, punctuality, and a determination to serve others well. When he dried the tears of frustration that sometimes blurred the words in my first books, he used to say ``Things take time.'' They still do, Dad.

Section II
Methodology

Motivating Students to Actively Engage in Reading

by William H. Rupley, Michael J. Ash,
and Timothy R. Blair

Motivating students to read is recognized as an important variable at all levels of reading instruction. A major concern of teachers is how to motivate students to actively engage in learning the basic reading skills, applying these skills in their reading, and reading for personal enjoyment. A major feature that facilitates the success of developmental, corrective, and remedial reading instruction is the teacher's ability to motivate students.

Quite often, however, teachers labor under the unfortunate assumption that the major task of motivating students to read can be accomplished by providing activities aimed at making reading more fun or interesting. The efficacy of such an approach is questionable, precisely because students differ in how they react to such activities. Some students may approach the task with enthusiasm, others may avoid it entirely, and some may be indifferent about it; these differences are illustrative of what is meant by the concept of motivation.

What then do we know about motivation, and how is it that we apply that knowledge to reading instruction? Frustratingly, there are many theories of human motivation, but few attempts have been made to apply these theories to the teaching of reading. However, research and the expert opinions of psychologists interested in motivation offer a theoretical foundation on which reading educators can build.

Deci (1975) has grouped the widely varied notions of motivation into two broad classifications: (1) *mechanistic* concepts of motivation that emphasize the impact of past and current environmental influences and (2) *organismic* concepts of motivation that stress the internal or intrinsic factors of motivation.

MECHANISTIC MOTIVATION

Psychologists who prefer mechanistic concepts of motivation are prone to talk to teachers about "motivating kids." Mechanists emphasize the use of praise and reward systems to facilitate and support reading behaviors. Also, there is a primary concern for the scheduling and sequencing of activities, and a strong effort is made to make learning as errorless as possible.

Mechanistic theories are extremely optimistic about the ability of *teachers* to enhance a pupil's motivation for the reading task. Through the use of properly scheduled reinforcement, aided by a carefully sequenced curriculum, the reading teacher can "shape" a pupil's responses until they approximate the identified learning product.

While the mechanistic approach has recorded some impressive successes in the teaching of reading (e.g., Sullivan and Distar), some problems have arisen. Often it is difficult to adequately define the behavioral goals that are truly of interest. Hence, the defined goals are often seen as trivial or so specific to a particular behavior that they are deemed irrelevant. Moreover, teachers sometimes have difficulty finding effective reinforcers to use in consequenting behavior. Nevertheless, mechanistic notions of motivation have proved to be an effective model for building and maintaining children's reading behaviors, particularly in low-interest activities that lack self-sustaining properties.

ORGANISMIC THEORIES OF MOTIVATION

As was true with our discussion of behavioristic notions of motivation, organismic theories take many forms, but certain underlying assumptions allow us to effectively describe them. Organismic approaches differ primarily from mechanistic ones by focusing on the role of cognitive and/or affective processes as determiners of behavior. Humans' thoughts and feelings determine the lawful and ordered way they act on their environment (Deci, 1975). Notice that the emphasis here is on factors occurring inside the organism, in contrast to the mechanist's focus on external factors.

Thus, the advice concerning classroom motivation derived from organismic theories exhorts teachers to focus on the inherent motivations of children. For example, White (1959) has proposed that motivation is an expression of an inborn need to be effective or competent. We are thus driven to seek new information, to make sense of it in terms of what we know, and then seek still more. The task of teachers, then, is to match the demands of instruction to the past cognitive experiences of each child (Hunt, 1961).

A second motivational component in organismic theories is affect or feelings. While the exact role of affect in the motivational process is not agreed upon, the role of emotions in organismic theories of motivation lies in both stimuli for action and antecedents of goal directed behavior. Ausubel and Robinson (1969) stated:

> Since teachers are constantly exhorted to attend to the child's needs, interests, and abilities, it is no doubt useful for teachers to be acquainted with these general need systems. If a hierarchy concept has any validity, such knowledge is important because a child in the classroom may be attempting to satisfy some prepotent need when the teacher is attempting to activate the desire to know and understand (p. 355).

Abraham Maslow (1943), a motivation theorist and psychologist, proposed a theory of motivation founded on human needs. Maslow developed a hierarchy of needs consisting of the following five levels: physiological, safety, love and belonging, self-esteem, and self-actualization. He viewed these needs in a prepotency fashion where one need essentially occupies an individual's attention until satisfied. After a need is adequately satisfied, the next prepotent need arises. While the concern of this article is on increasing cognitive abilities, which are in the self-actualization stage, the interdependency of all human needs will not and

should not be ignored. Reading is not just a mechanical tool to be learned, it is an intricate part of the entire person; affected by his/her needs, attitudes, self-concept, and emotions.

Crucial to understanding organismic approaches is the awareness that feelings condition cognitive thoughts. Feelings can hinder or aid intellectual development, and this inter-relatedness must be seized upon by the classroom teacher. Rubin (1973) stated:

> Children's perceptions, and the emotions they attach to these perceptions, once recognized by the teacher, can be used with telling effect to better understand the child and to invent learning activities that facilitate cognitive growth, that enhance emotional stability, and that strike at the very heart of what the child considers relevant (p. 15).

Applications of Motivation Theories in Reading Instruction

Research has shown that teachers use signs of student attention and interest in judging their effectiveness (Jackson, 1968). Perhaps intuitively, teachers know that motivation is a precursor to learning. But as is often the case, knowing how to acquire such motivation is not so intuitively obvious. Earlier it was pointed out that attempts to motivate students by only using activities perceived by the teacher to be interesting may not maximize their motivation. Motivation activities aimed at the whole class or even groups of students often overlook the value that an individual associates with the activity. For example, reading activities centered around puppet plays, role playing activities, games, etc. may not be highly valued by all of the students. It is possible, also, that even though all the students appear interested and motivated by an activity, only a few of them are actually motivated to actively engage in learning the desired reading behavior. Thus, the teacher perceives the high interest level of a few students to be reflective of the majority, when in fact the majority of the students may be neutral.

One could argue that it is possible to motivate a large group of students with a specific interesting activity; however, an important concern is whether or not the students are motivated to acquire the desired reading behavior. For example, a puppet play could motivate all students in a group to actively participate in the play. That is, all of the students find the production of the play appealing and are actively engaged in some part of it. This active participation could suggest that all students are learning and each values this learning. A rival explanation that must be considered by teachers is that the play does not demand active engagement in learning the identified reading behavior. Furthermore, the appeal of the activity could in fact preclude students' learning of the desired reading behavior identified by the teacher.

The above-mentioned concerns are not intended to suggest that teachers discontinue their efforts to capture students' interest and channel it to motivate active engagement in reading. What we are recommending is that teachers be more aware of what does actually interest individual students. A logical first step in motivating students' engagement in reading instruction is arousing them to actively participate in instruction that will lead to the acquisition of valued reading behaviors. On one hand, many beginning reading tasks lack immediate relevancy for the students, and as such are not amenable to a personal motivation scheme. Associating letters with the sounds they represent and learning to recognize words on sight are examples of reading activities toward which many children may be neutral. On the other hand, teachers can enhance students' motivation toward such beginning reading tasks by noting how they react to them. Setting specific purposes for learning, illustrating the application of reading skills in meaningful comprehension tasks, building in small, highly related instruction steps, and making students aware of their progress in reading for meaning, are possible means for increasing the relevancy of reading tasks and, thus, enhancing motivation (Anderson, Everston, Brophy, 1979; Heilman, Blair, and Rupley, 1981).

Many teachers are aware of the need to support students' reading behaviors extrinsically because of the fact that all students are not motivated by all things in the classroom at any given point in time. Our earlier reference to interesting activities aimed at a large number of students supports this concept. In a practical sense, such teachers recognize the value in extrinsically motivating students. Extrinsic approaches combine motivation with the desired learning outcomes and the focus is on reading behaviors in relation to motivational strategies that will enhance students' engagement in learning. If a student does not demonstrate the desired learning behavior, then teachers evaluate either the motivation schemes, the instruction, or both. Based on this evaluation, appropriate adjustments can be made to accommodate students' needs and enhance their participation in learning.

MOTIVATION GUIDELINES AND EVALUATION

Evaluation of the effects of motivation strategies on students' reading appears to be the key to successfully motivating learning. Regardless of whether one leans toward an intrinsic or an extrinsic approach in motivating classroom reading, attention to how the approach influences learning should be assessed. Some basic evaluation concerns related to motivation and reading instruction are presented below.

1. Students who actively participate in a reading activity because they find it interesting and meaningful will probably not show increased engagement if an extrinsic reward is employed. In many cases, the introduction of an extrinsic reward will decrease students' motivation in a task they find interesting. The use of extrinsic rewards may best be delayed as long as students' interest persists. However, if engagement in the task begins to decrease, teachers may wish to introduce some extrinsic rewards to re-stimulate students' interest.

2. Participation in low interest reading tasks may be enhanced by extrinsic motivation strategies. The effects of extrinsic rewards will probably decrease in sustaining students' engagement over varying time periods. That is, students may begin to associate less value with a reward as it is used over any length of time. Attending closely to how extrinsic motivators are sustaining desired reading behaviors will enable teachers to make necessary adjustment in terms of students' active participation.

3. It appears that the lack of appropriate reinforcers is more damaging to intrinsic motivation than is their use (Bates, 1979). In terms of classroom reading instruction this suggests that for tasks where students already have developed some association with extrinsic rewards, lack of these rewards could negatively influence their motivation. Some reading tasks in which students engage could be both interesting and extrinsically rewarded. Therefore, students' own interests in the activity and extrinsic rewards provided by the teacher motivate them. If extrinsic rewards are removed or changed substantially, students' motivation could be negatively affected. Careful attention to evaluating the interaction of rewards with students' interest in terms of specific reading tasks is essential to continued motivation.

4. Not all reading behavior is associated with concrete rewards. Social reward systems, such as group membership, public praise, and peer recognition can positively affect students' motivation in reading if they

associate value with these social factors. Teachers can provide opportunities within their classrooms for social reward systems to function. Close monitoring of how students respond to such systems is recommended to determine how they impact students' motivation.

SUMMARY

A concern for student motivation should pervade all aspects of reading instruction. Instructional concerns for motivating students to read must go beyond just making learning fun or interesting. Dispelling the notion that all students are motivated by such a casual approach is the first step in viewing motivation as that which affects an individual's behavior as he strives to attain a goal.

The second step toward a pervasive concern for motivating students to read is approaching the development of reading instructional tasks in an analytical fashion. Analytical concerns for motivation in reading instruction can be facilitated by evaluating students' engagement in a reading activity in relation to motivational strategies that are employed. How students respond to reading tasks is often a result of their motivation. Teachers of reading who evaluate the effects of intrinsic and extrinsic means of motivation can make informed decisions for increased student involvement and learning.

REFERENCES

Anderson, L. M., Everston, C. M., & Brophy, J. E. An experimental study of effective teaching in first-grade reading groups. *Elementary School Journal,* 1979, *79,* 193–223.

Ausubel, D. P., & Robinson, F. G. *School learning: An introduction to educational psychology.* New York: Holt, Rinehart, and Winston, 1969.

Bates, J. A. Extrinsic reward and intrinsic motivation: A review with implications for the classroom. *Review of Educational Research,* 1979, *49,* 557–576.

Deci, L. *Intrinsic motivation.* New York: Plenum Press, 1975.

De Vries, D. L., & Edwards, J. *Expectancy theory and cooperation-competition in the classroom.* Paper presented at the Annual convention of the American Psychological Association, New Orleans, Louisiana, August 30, 1974.

Heilman, A., Blair, T. R., & Rupley, W. H. *Principles and practices of teaching reading.* Columbus, Ohio: Charles E. Merrill, 1981.

Hunt, J. M. *Intelligence and experience.* New York: Ronald Press, 1961.

Jackson, P. *Life in the classroom.* New York: Holt, Rinehart, and Winston, 1968.

Maslow, A. H. A theory of human motivation. *Psychological Review,* 1943, *50,* 370–396.

Rubin, J. *Facts and feelings in the classroom.* New York: The Viking Press, 1973.

White, R. W. Motivation reconsidered: The concept of competence. *Psychological Review,* 1959, *66,* 297–333.

Motivating Reluctant Readers: A Gentle Push

by Hilary Taylor Holbrook

Young people who cannot read at all are far outnumbered by young people who can read (poorly or well) but won't. The latter, who choose not to read, for whatever reason, have little advantage over those who are illiterate (Earle, ED 198 491; Joseph and Wittig, ED 192 276). Motivating students' interest in reading in the schools poses a two-sided challenge: rekindling a desire to read in those who have already established a pattern of avoiding reading situations, and igniting a lifelong reading interest in children learning to read *before* they become reading casualties. The following article examines materials in the ERIC system that address the problem of reluctant readers: the causes and indications of reading reluctance, some broad approaches to reading instruction that will introduce children to reading in a positive manner and alleviate potential problems, and finally, sources for specific activities to encourage young children in early reading efforts and reengage those students already exhibiting problems or disinterest.

CAUSES FOR RELUCTANCE

Somewhere along the educational path, the reluctant reader was left behind. Such a student's reluctance to read is either a disguise for poor reading skills, or an indication that reading never attracted the student's attention enough for him or her to develop adequate skills. In some cases, usually in the middle grades and up, the student can read well, but neither enjoys it nor appreciates its value. Whatever the reason, the result is an avoidance of any reading task. Sometimes a child will announce, "this is dumb" or "I'm not gonna do this stuff" in response to a reading task, or will engage in other off-task activities. During oral reading activities, a child may intentionally lose his or her place, or complain of hurting eyes or headaches. All of these behaviors are sending out messages of avoidance (Michael, EJ 238 462).

The causes of reading reluctance are as varied as the individuals who will not read. Probably the most important factor for consideration is that, for some students, learning to read is a risky business. According to Arleen Michael (EJ 238 462), when a child is decoding aloud, he or she "makes incorrect responses, often does not know what is expected, what is correct or incorrect, and exposes these inadequacies to the view of peers and teachers." It is essentially a guessing game. If a decoding error is corrected aloud by the teacher, the child's efforts are immediately and publicly judged as wrong. Repeated experiences with this kind of failure result in frustration, and eventually, anxiety over reading itself.

Beverly Farr (ED 198 491) suggests that emphasis on isolated skills during reading instruction precipitates reading problems.

> The fear that children will not learn all the basic skills prompts teachers to use a variety of materials and activities which endorse the practice of isolated skills and the belief that such practices will lead to better reading . . . as a consequence of skill-oriented instruction or an overemphasis on word recognition, some children are lured

away from the idea that reading is a meaning getting process. They see reading as a ''subject,'' one in which they are continually meeting failure.

Other factors Farr believes contribute to reading reluctance include a lack of sufficient background information (schemata) to enable a child to deal with the concepts, situations, or events included in the reading materials, and materials that are meaningless and do not command a child's attention because they are not personally important.

Once a child begins to register a reluctance toward reading, a teacher may subconsciously label him or her as a problem reader, although the child may have developed some profitable strategies to cope with reading. Assigned reading groups seldom provide mobility for a child with weaker skills, and may even establish or reinforce a cycle of failure and avoidance—the child becomes a self-fulfilling failure.

Children's reading behavior can also be affected by their perceptions of the reading attitudes of others. The results of a survey of reading attitudes showed that while 100 percent of male teachers regarded reading as a masculine activity, 100 percent of the female teachers, two-thirds of the fathers and sons, and almost all of the mothers and daughters regarded reading as a feminine activity (Filangieri, ED 169 506).

TEACHING APPROACHES TO SOLVING THE PROBLEM

Catching reading problems before they occur calls for a shift in both perceptions of the reading process and attitude toward reading errors, and a change in the materials used for reading instruction. According to Murlee Hart (ED 172 150), reading teachers need to look upon errors as clues to the child's system of logic, rather than a sign of lack of intelligence. A policy of encouragement during the early reading process (similar to the indulgent attitude accorded children during the early stages of language acquisition), will create an environment in which the child is relaxed and willing to take risks.

A successful remedial program must be structured in such a way that the risks the child is asked to take are those that can be managed. A gradual increase in the risk taking should be built into the structure of the reading task until the child is able to deal successfully with the risks

inherent in a traditional reading session (Michael, EJ 238 462).

Four experiments reported by Mark Lepper (ED 135 466) focused on the ways children could be trained to imitate others in imposing on themselves higher performance standards in game situations. The results indicated that children who observed peer models exhibiting high or low standards of self-reward imitated those standards. The implications of these results where reading motivation is concerned suggest that reluctant or slow readers would show marked achievement and interest if they observed their peers modeling strong skills and interest. (They also suggest that isolating poor readers in remedial classes, away from better peer models, may be a self-defeating approach.) A great deal of subtlety and tact is required of teachers in drawing children's attention to peer models, as well as a teaching policy of enthusiastic encouragement (as opposed to comparison).

Reading in combination with other activities teaches children that reading is not an isolated task. ''Learning to Read through the Arts'' (ED 186 863), a Title One program implemented in New York City, reinforces specific reading skills in combination with artistic and creative activities. For example, after reading a story, a student may draw or paint a picture of a scene in the story, or depict his or her impressions of the story. In addition to improving retention, this teaching method works as a springboard to motivate further reading on topics of interest and encourages personal responses to the reading materials.

Reading materials, probably the most critical factor in developing reading skills and interest, should be suited to each child. Award-winning children's literature that children themselves might choose to read is likely to engage their interest in reading far more than commercial reading series, and it, too, can be used as a springboard to further reading in subject areas or by the same authors (Washburn, ED 151 804; Thomas and Loring, ED 181 439). Monroe Cohen's ''Excellent Paperbacks for Children'' (ED 178 199) is but one of the many booklists of titles recommended for children. Sometimes it takes only one good work to hook a child into a lifetime of reading or to rescue a child who is losing interest.

Incorporating newspapers, comics, and other materials that children come in contact with in their daily lives into the teaching routine is an approach that will emphasize the fact that reading can be fun and that it has a purpose, something that teaching skills in isolation often fails to do.

MOTIVATING ACTIVITIES

Many activities have been developed for the classroom to keep young readers interested in reading while developing higher level skills. Sheryl Joseph and Diane Wittig (ED 192 276) have compiled twenty-nine teaching ideas that emphasize reading as a pleasurable activity. These ideas include games, multimedia activities, and writing exercises that focus on survival reading materials, vocabulary extension, and skill reinforcement. In one such activity, children are asked to read the local newspaper edition from their birth date, and discuss what toys, movies, and other elements were popular, and how customs and activities have changed since then.

Michael Currier's ''Five Fingers: Games and Activities to Motivate the Growing Reader'' (ED 133 686) contains ninety-six classroom-tested ideas that motivate by encouraging students; they can develop and reinforce skills in word analysis, comprehension, and vocabulary in any basal or individualized reading programs. Chapters in ''Motivating Reluctant Readers,'' edited by Alfred J. Ciani (ED 198 491), also provide suggestions for working with students who function at a frustration level or have an aversion to reading, including using popular music, and motivating through improved self-concept.

For teachers in other subject areas, Ellen McManus et al. (ED 182 692) provides activities to integrate language arts with other subject areas including drama, science, photography, and career awareness. An example activity uses the reading of restaurant menus in a science class discussion of the four basic food groups to see how restaurants group their foods. These activities can prove particularly useful in reminding children that reading is not a separate subject but is an important process used in all subject areas.

Factors outside the classroom, particularly the home environment, may also have an impact on reading motivation. Exposure to reading aloud and to using the library will generate early reading interest in children. ''Developing Active Readers: Ideas for Parents, Teachers, and Librarians'' (ED 178 872) provides suggestions for selecting books, assessing reading interests, and taking children to the library. It also presents activities for using literature and oral reading and for using the media to spark an interest in reading in the content areas.

Finally, for groups wishing to establish reading motivation programs on a local level, the Smithsonian Institution has compiled a ''Resource Manual for Inexpensive Book Distribution Programs for Reading Motivation'' (ED 150 564). The manual includes information on building the program and the steps necessary to qualify for federal funding, on planning motivational activities and involving the community, and on selecting books that will arouse reading interest.

The educational path is wide enough and has sufficient branches and sideroads to accommodate all children. A fresh approach to the reading process, a positive attitude toward reading errors (students can learn from them) and a variety of activities that integrate isolated skills and present reading as a way to gather exciting and useful information could provide just the gentle nudges needed to keep many children from wandering off or getting left behind.

REFERENCES

Ciani, Alfred J., Ed. *Motivating Reluctant Readers.* Newark, DE: International Reading Association, 1981. 113 pp. (ED 198 491)

Cohen, Libby. ''Stereotyping of Learning Disabled and Remedial Reading Students by Teachers.'' Paper presented at the annual international convention of the Council for Exceptional Children, Philadelphia, PA, April 1980. 19 pp. (ED 187 045)

Cohen, Monroe D., Ed. ''Excellent Paperbacks for Children.'' Washington, DC: Association for Childhood Education International, 1979. 57 pp. (ED 178 199)

Currier, Michael E. ''Five Fingers: Games and Activities to Motivate the Growing Reader.'' Paper presented at the annual meeting of the International Reading Association, Plains Regional Conference, Wichita, KS, March 1976. 115 pp. (ED 133 686)

Earle, Richard A. ''Foreword.'' In *Motivating Reluctant Readers,* edited by Alfred J. Ciani. Newark, DE: International Reading Association, 1981. 113 pp. (ED 198 491)

Farr, Beverly P. ''Building Language Experiences for Reluctant Readers.'' In *Motivating Reluctant Readers,* edited by Alfred J. Ciani. Newark, DE: International Reading Association, 1981. 113 pp. (ED 198 491)

Filangieri, Jerry S. ''A Survey on Reading as a Highly Masculine or Highly Feminine Activity.'' Master's thesis, Kean College of New Jersey, 1979. 18 pp. (ED 169 506)

Hart, Murlee M. ''Preventing the Proliferation of Problem Readers.'' Paper presented at the annual meeting of the National Council of Teachers of English, Kansas City, MO, November 1978. 11 pp. (ED 172 150)

Joseph, Sheryl and Wittig, Diane L. M., Eds. ''Reading Remedies for Involving the Reluctant Reader.'' Compiled at a special 1980 summer reading workshop, Lehigh University, Bethlehem, PA, 1980. 13 pp. (ED 192 276)

Koenke, Karl. ''ERIC/RCS Report: Motivation and Reading.'' *Language Arts* 55 (November/December 1978): 998–1002. (EJ 190 334)

Learning to Read through the Arts. Brooklyn, NY: New York City Board of Education, Division of Curriculum and Instruction, 1980. 17 pp. (ED 186 863)

Lepper, Mark R. "Generalized Effects of Modeled Self-Reinforcement Training. Final Report." Prepared at the Department of Psychology, Stanford University, Stanford, CA, 1976. 53 pp. (ED 135 466).

Lidstone, John, Comp. "Reading Improvement through the Arts." Albany, NY: New York State Education Department, 1979. 26 pp. (ED 178 899)

McManus, Ellen; Gosselin, Donna-Jean; and Proulx, Karen. *I Did It, I Said It, I Wrote It, I Read It: A Language Experience Approach to Reading.* Harrisville, RI: Burrillville School Department, 1979. 24 pp. (ED 182 692)

Michael, Arleen. "Reading and Risk Taking: The Teacher's Role." *Reading Horizons* 21 (Winter 1981): 139–142. (EJ 238 452)

Monson, Dianne L. and McClenathan, DayAnn K., Eds. *Developing Active Readers: Ideas for Parents, Teachers, and Librarians.* Newark, DE: International Reading Association, 1979. 112 pp. (ED 178 872)

Myers, Betty; Cruickshank, Donald R.; and Rentel, Victor M. "Perceived Problems of Teachers of Reading: Fact and Paradox." Study prepared at Ohio State University, 1975. 66 pp. (ED 167 951)

"Resource Manual for Inexpensive Book Distribution Programs for Reading Motivation." Washington, DC: Smithsonian Institution, National Reading Is Fundamental Program, 1977. 36 pp. (ED 150 564)

Thomas, James L. and Loring, Ruth M., Eds. *Motivating Children and Young Adults to Read.* Phoenix, AZ: Oryx Press, 1980. 189 pp. (ED 181 439)

Washburn, Judith S. "Motivating Lifetime Readers of Literature." Paper presented at the annual meeting of the National Council of Teachers of English, New York, NY, November 1977. 16 pp. (ED 151 804)

Helping More Students Become Mature Readers

by Norma B. Kahn

Many English teachers and reading specialists would probably agree that two related goals for their teaching should be motivating more students to become lifetime readers and helping more students become mature readers. In the February 1974 issue of *The English Journal* I proposed some ways to accomplish the first goal; here I propose some ways to accomplish the second. After describing what I believe are six characteristics of mature readers, I will suggest how English teachers and reading specialists might help more students develop these characteristics.

In my opinion, mature readers:
1. enjoy choosing their own reading material
2. turn versatilely from one type of reading material to another
3. respond to the material they read in appropriate ways
4. remember what they read sufficiently for their purposes
5. try consciously to learn new words
6. concentrate when they read.

How can English teachers and reading specialists help more students become mature readers?

1. If mature readers enjoy choosing for themselves reading material which will meet their needs or purposes, then we should give students frequent opportunity to consider their individual interests and to choose reading material to meet them. An elective curriculum (or elective units within courses for a traditional curriculum) is especially helpful toward this end, and some categories for elective courses or units are directly appropriate toward it: coping with problems or challenges in living; language, what it is and how it works or means; broadening interests; improving study skills.

For example, a course or unit on survival can offer students a choice of interpretation of the word survival (academic, economic, physical, emotional). For the subject of physical survival, choice of materials can include the most recent editions of first aid books at several levels of difficulty (the Boy Scout handbook, the Red Cross handbook, Bantam's *New Essential First Aid,* by A. Ward Gardner and Peter J. Roylance); fiction and non-fiction that dramatize efforts to survive in physically threatening situations; accounts written by the students themselves about their own encounters with physical danger. Experts on the subject can be consulted regarding specific questions and about related reading material. Librarians can be invited to give book talks to inform and interest students about particular books on the subject; more important, librarians can help students learn to find appropriate materials in their libraries.

With students who have had little previous experience in making choices for themselves to meet their needs and purposes, the number of choices might have to be limited initially, perhaps to only a few elective units or courses and to only a few books.

2. If mature readers can turn versatilely from one type of reading material to another, reading each in ways appropriate for their purposes and for the nature of the reading material, we should, in discussing each new reading assignment:
—help students learn to determine quickly the particular nature of the reading material (for

expository material, studying organizational aids like the summary and conclusion; for narrative material, reading the opening pages);

—suggest that students decide consciously, having determined the particular nature of the material, whether or not they should read it further at all and, if they decide to read it, to decide their purposes for reading it;

—encourage students to read with their purposes in mind—and to be aware that they may find in the material values beyond their original purposes;

—reassure students that all reading need not be consciously purposeful, just as all traveling and all meetings with people need not be consciously purposeful. There will be many times when reading expository material might be like heading west without a map—for the sheer pleasure of it; and reading narrative might be like meeting someone unexpectedly, without plan or purpose.

Figure 1 presents several analogies I have found helpful to students in developing reading versatility. (See also my "Using Analogies to Help Students Become Versatile Readers," *Clearing House*, March 1978.)

Figure 1. Before Reading at Length Preview, or Meet Your Book, *Briefly*

Reading non-fiction	is like	driving
Therefore		
previewing before reading unfamiliar non-fiction	is like	studying a map before driving to an unfamiliar place
Reading fiction	is like	meeting someone new
Therefore		
reading the opening pages of fiction before deciding whether to read on (and on)	is like	spending a few minutes with someone new before deciding whether to meet again (and again)

3. Mature readers respond to reading material in ways appropriate for their purposes and for the nature of the material; so we should help students understand the differences between various kinds of material—especially between imaginative literature and expository

prose, help them discover ways that each kind might meet various purposes, and give them opportunities to try responding to each in a variety of ways.

For students with little experience in reading imaginative literature, we should introduce them to if not with adult classics, but with adolescent novels that involve experiences familiar to them and that are relatively simple in form. For these students and others, we should include with any study of literature many opportunities to read simply for pleasure, simply to enter the world of the book without any overt response required.

After students preview exposition or read the opening pages of narrative, a question like "What in this material is important to *me?*" can help them connect the material with their previous experiences and knowledge and can increase their interest in and understanding of the material.

For exposition, students can be helped to develop more critical questions, such as "What in this material does the author regard as most important and how can I tell? Is the argument logical? Is the evidence convincing? How does the material compare to other material I know on the same subject?" For imaginative literature or any narrative, students can be helped to develop questions which can increase what Alan Purves has called "engagement-involvement" ("What does this material cause me to feel or imagine?"), perception ("What in the material caused me to feel or imagine as I did?"), interpretation ("considering all the elements of the material, what does it seem to mean?"), and evaluation ("What is the value of the material to me personally, and what might be its value for others?").

When we ask students to respond overtly, we should give some choice of ways to respond: small-group discussions; readers' theatre or creative dramatics or role-playing; appropriate action (in a unit on physical survival, perhaps enroll in a course on the Heimlich maneuver for choking victims, or a course in cardio-pulmonary resuscitation for victims of heart attack or drowning, or write a letter to authorities to urge correction of specific dangerous conditions).

4. Mature readers remember what they read sufficiently for their purposes; so we should:

—encourage students to consider the relationship of what they are reading to what they already know or think about the subject (thus consciously to develop stronger concepts);

—teach students the value of "chunking"—determining the internal organization of expository material, learning the basic units chunk by chunk (the greater the detail to be learned, the smaller the chunk) by reciting the chunk aloud from memory or working a related problem or creating a related graphic representation;

—help students discover the value of carefully selective notetaking, for learning more in less time.

5. Mature readers try consciously to learn new words or new meanings of familiar words, as part of their broader interest in language and its effective use; so we should provide many kinds of encouragement for this:

—teach vocabulary systematically (using guides such as *Techniques for Teaching Vocabulary,* by Edgar Dale et al.), preferably in a course or unit on some aspect of language;

—teach vocabulary incidentally also, for example by helping students find and share occasionally the origins of words that they consider interesting;

—assign learning of words chosen primarily from the students' own vocabulary collections: students can note any unfamiliar words they encounter and the phrase in which they find them, research the words after they finish the reading, and turn in for an accuracy check all of their research notes.

6. Mature readers concentrate when they read, controlling when necessary and possible the factors that affect concentration (the physical environment and their own mental and physical state); so we should:

—encourage students, in previewing, to consider the difficulty of the material (Are there many abstractions or unfamiliar concepts? Is the organization less than clear? Is the type too small? Are the lines too long?), and if necessary to find a less difficult or more readable book on the subject;

—encourage students to develop their background in the subject about which they want to read—by first-hand experience when this is practical, by using audio-visual materials or talking with experts on the subject, or by reading introductory or less difficult material first;

—provide information about emotional, mental and physical states that often affect concentration and ways to change these states (getting more sleep or exercise, getting better ventilation or light, eating more regularly more appropriate food, dealing with distractions in the environment, seeking counseling about personal problems.)

Figure 2 is an outline that I have found useful for class discussion on the subject of improving concentration.

Figure 2. Suggestions for Improving Concentration on Reading and Study

A. Prepare to concentrate.

  1. Avoid, or cope with in advance of studying, factors which are likely to reduce concentration:
    a. Anxiety
      —about whether assignments will be completed on time.
      —about whether you are doing the assignments correctly.
    b. Other emotional distractions.
    c. Physical distractions.
    d. Fatigue.

  2. Provide for factors which increase concentration:
    a. Build your background in the subject matter to be studied.
    b. Increase your interest in the subject.
    c. In reading expository material (*not* imaginative literature) impress upon your memory the organization of the major units to be read *before* trying to read and learn the parts which compose the units: then learn one part at a time. (In other words, chew and swallow one bite before taking another bite.)

B. Study actively.

C. Use time-saving techniques, to shorten the time in which you must concentrate.

If mature readers have these six characteristics and more, is there any way that we can help students realize how all of these characteristics can interrelate? Perhaps the best way is for English teachers and reading specialists to be models for students; that is, for us to demonstrate that we are mature readers ourselves.

BIBLIOGRAPHY

Altick, Richard. *Preface to Critical Reading*. 5th ed. New York: Holt, Rinehart, 1969.

Coger, Leslie and Melvin White. *Readers Theatre Handbook*. Rev. ed. Glenview, Ill.: Scott Foresman, 1973.

Dale, Edgar et al. *Techniques for Teaching Vocabulary*. Chicago: Field Enterprises, 1971.

Henry, George. *Teaching Reading as Concept Development*. Newark, Del.: International Reading Association, 1974.

Kahn, Norma B. ''A Proposal for Motivating More Students to Lifetime Reading of Literature.'' *The English Journal* 63 (Feb. 1974), 34–43.

————. *More Learning in Less Time*. Rochelle Park, N.J.: Hayden, 1979.

————. ''Using Analogies to Help Students Become Versatile Readers.'' *Clearing House* 51 (March 1978), 329–34.

Norman, Donald A. *Memory and Attention*. 2nd ed. New York: Wiley, 1976.

Purves, Alan. *How Porcupines Make Love: Notes on a Response-Centered Curriculum*. Lexington, Mass.: Xerox College Publishing, 1972.

Shirley, Fehl. ''Influence of Reading on Concepts, Attitudes, and Behavior.'' *Journal of Reading*, 12 (Feb. 1969), 369–72. Also in *Teaching Reading for Human Values in High School*, James Duggins, ed. Columbus, Ohio: Merrill, 1972.

Reaching the Able but Unwilling Reader

by Elana Rabban

We are disturbed by the low level of literacy and writing ability in this country, and some attempts are being made to alter this situation. But are we equally disturbed about those top, high-school students who get the best SAT scores, who rank highest on the state's Regents exams, who get into the most prestigious colleges, but who read only in connection with course work, and admit they don't read at all for pleasure—or only rarely? What does this mean? Is it serious? Can we do something about those students who have never acquired the love of reading? Or college graduates who read an average of one novel a year?

What it means, I think, is that, not surprisingly, some of the ingredients which contribute to making outstanding students also pose challenges for librarians. It is not uncommon, for example, for some of our most able students to admit to not having time to read for pleasure and relaxation after having given their all to do well on tests and required papers. Similarly, an atmosphere of considerable pressure reduces the chances of experiencing the joy of learning, the leisure to read, the time to memorize a poem (if not required), and the indulgence of not putting an engrossing book aside until it is finished.

Is it serious? Yes, I think it is. Admittedly, it is less serious than the inability to read. But educators' preoccupation with test scores and entrance examinations as the measure for getting ahead has discouraged the passion for exploration. The range of personal reading choice has been seriously diminished. The possibility of discovering the real and lasting pleasure of reading, based in the confidence of one's own judgment and taste, has been reduced. Providing the time, both in and out of school, to pursue reading for relaxation and fun is not a prime concern.

Are these unreasonable expectations? After all, with the majority of schools teaching how to read, what arrogance it is to insist that those who *can* read should *want* to read. Perhaps. But isn't this just the point? Are not skills meant for pleasures they can provide? What use is a Rolls Royce sitting in a garage, a Rembrandt not viewed, a feast not eaten, a wine not tasted, a book not enjoyed?

Does this imply lowering our high academic standards? In a world that is tough and competitive, can we allow our best students to read for fun and pleasure?

The answer is, yes! Librarians and educators can begin by dispelling the dilemma that maintaining standards is necessarily and always in opposition to pleasure and enjoyment. (A Puritan ethic of doubtful value.) Furthermore, we can acknowledge that we live in a world where competition reigns, but we do not need to reinforce its most damaging aspects. Librarians can, in a properly managed library, which is less formal and less structured than a classroom and which does not evaluate and compare students, give full rein to acquiring the love and fun of reading. To do this, we must have an abundance and variety of reading materials— the easy, the more demanding, the classic, the new, the serious, the frivolous, the hardcovers, and the thousands of paperbacks—everywhere. We must avoid being judgmental; we must not put down students whose reading choices do not meet our personal expectations. We must not recommend books because they will impress parents nor vie with the English course list. We must not recommend books to enhance our image as one that is elitist and sophisticated. We must genuinely love books *and* students and believe it our mission to bring them together. We must believe that in addition to librarians, teachers, and parents there are students out there who—given good guidance and ample choice—will respond favorably. Our conviction about quality books must be conveyed with a light touch. We must work with faculty and administrators to arrange the school day for periods of quiet reading, for reading aloud, and for being read to. We must discourage an attitude on the part of faculty members that, in assignment homework, *more* is *better*. Much of homework is busy work to fill up the free time of students who could better be enjoying (yes, relaxing with) a book. We must also work with parents to encourage them to read, and we must work with community groups to upgrade reading—to make it ''in,'' to make the writer (or the poet) a hero and a role model.

Will this help? I can't be sure. But librarians must keep trying. If we do not, there is the implicit arrogance that is more dangerous—that we are the chosen few who enjoy reading because of our higher intelligence, diligence, and superior taste. We are, in fact, the fortunate ones who were exposed to a teacher or librarian with a sense of mission, who lived in an era of fewer distractions, at a time when family life was more stable, when children witnessed parents reading more frequently. We cannot and should not turn the clock back. Powerful forces are at work creating an environment not ideally suited to leisure reading. All the more reason that, despite all the other distractions, we feel it's our mission to make reading both fun and a source of enjoyment and relaxation for those who *can* read but *don't*.

Reading Made Necessary, Naturally!

by Larry M. Arnoldsen

In the many years I've been a teacher, I have not given one textbook assignment, one homework assignment, or one test. But I believe few teachers have had their students do more reading or more learning outside of the school. I decided a long time ago to avoid doing things that students associated with a lot of pain. I learned not to use words like "text," "exam," "term paper," and "homework."

I remember announcing to my high school students at the first of the year that I didn't believe in term papers; they cheered with relief. They didn't notice that before the term was over they had done more than the equivalent of a dozen term papers. I remember them cheering when I said there would be no text assignments. But when the term was over, they had read the equivalent of three or four texts.

How was this accomplished? I turned around the typical pattern. We typically say, "Read chapter 1." So the students read, or try. After a while maybe they don't read at all. Next we discuss the chapter, until we realize the students haven't read the chapter. At that point we may read it aloud as a class and then discuss it, pointing out how important it is to the students and their lives. Then we have a test or answer the questions at the end of the chapter.

Another typical pattern is to assign the chapter and the questions at the end before discussing it. "Poor" students do neither the questions nor the reading. "Good" students usually do only the questions.

A PARKING LOT, THE TEACHERS' HANDBOOK, AND THE CIVIL WAR

I believe it is better to begin with the questions than with the reading, but not the questions at the end of the chapter. Texts don't ask the right questions. The right questions are more thought provoking than the ones usually found at the end of a chapter. Questions such as "Is justice for the rich?" "Is democracy good?" "If you could create a world, would you have flies on it?" "Is war good?" you usually don't find at the end of the chapter.

The best questions teachers rarely ask. They're not in books and are often not known to the teachers. The students know the right questions to get learning and reading going. Some time ago I was teaching U.S. history in a high school in California. My classes often met in the library. One day when I entered the library, a good portion of my third period class was congregated around a table having a rap session. I joined them; they continued without particularly noticing me.

What the students were having was a gripe session. It was more than that—it was a planning session. They were planning how to avoid a possible new school rule: "All student vehicles must be placed in the authorized parking lot, there to remain until the end of the school day." They would not be able to use their cars during the noon hour. As I listened to the discussion, the wheels began to spin and I wondered how the parking lot might become a U.S. history concern.

These students were in this particular class on the basis of their academic records in social studies. They were "C" students and most were resistant and unresponsive to "traditional" subject matter. We were in the second or third month of the year and I had not been successful in getting them to learn much history. My search for an alternative to traditional education had proved unsuccessful with this type of student. I had for a number of years been experimenting with enjoyable learning activities that had resulted in very sophisticated and significant learning for my students, and I had been successful with "A" and "B" students, but with those below that grade point I had largely failed.

As I listened to the talk and wondered what to do, I was interrupted by one of the students asking me if I agreed with this rule. I responded that it didn't matter much whether I agreed or not, that if I were at the school the next year and were assigned to police or enforce the proposed rule, I would do so because of my contractual obligation. The student continued with, "Yes, but do you *agree*?" At this point it became obvious to me that there were greater and deeper issues at stake than automobiles or parking lots. It also became evident to me that these greater issues were the stuff that history and life were made of. If this parking lot thing were related to greater issues, then history could have value for these students. Why not probe history to help shed light on this issue so important to my students?

Later that day I noticed a circular listing some films being shown around the high school that week. One being used by the English department, called "The Trial and Execution of Socrates," turned out to be one of the series of television specials called "You Are There." It was extremely well done with outstanding actors. A little more thinking resulted in a plan I thought worth trying.

The next day as the students entered the classroom, they noticed the projector and film and asked the usual question, "Say, are we going to have a film today?"

"Yes," I said, "that is if you still want to talk about the parking lot problem."

They did. I told them I thought the film had a direct bearing on the issues. After the film, we discussed Socrates' problem. Socrates found himself subject to the application of a rule to which he did not agree. We discussed his decision. We discussed the similarity between him and them. We discussed what his position on the parking lot issue might have been. The bell rang. Class was over.

Next day as the class entered the room and became seated, I asked them if they wanted to talk about the parking lot issue again. They did. I told them I would like to read them a few lines. I read some from Thoreau's *Civil Disobedience*. We discussed Thoreau and compared him with Socrates and the parking lot issue. We speculated about the kind of conversation those two might have, especially as it related to the parking lot. The bell rang. Class was over.

The next day I asked if they wanted to talk about the parking lot. They did. I asked what seemed to be the central issue of the American Revolution. They suggested a problem about some rules. We talked about what some of the founders of the United States had to say about rules and how that related to them. We discussed what the patriots might say on the parking lot issue. The bell rang. Class was over.

The next day they said, "Hey, let's talk some more about the parking lot."

I asked them, "What was the central issue of the American Civil War?"

They agreed, "Some rules." We had talked again about the relationship of that event and the parking lot. The bell rang. Class was over.

The next day as the students entered the room, they seemed unusually quiet. I sat on my desk and looked the class over. They continued to sit, quietly and seemingly tired, looking back at me. I asked them if they wanted to talk about the parking lot issue again.

One of them said to me, "Well, Mr. Arnoldsen, you win, but we sure feel helpless!" I was quite puzzled with this statement and said that I didn't understand.

He continued by saying, "Well, look, you've convinced us that we shouldn't take the law into our own hands, so to speak. That if the rule is that we mustn't remove our cars from the parking lot during the school day next year, we should accept that. But it seems so unfair. It seems like we ought to have *something* to say about it."

This was an interesting turn of events. I suppose that if my goal had been to teach "law and order" as it is normally thought of, I could consider myself quite successful. But that had not been my goal; my goal had been for them to see and experience some value to history. I had used the rule strategy because it was the most opportune. I had not anticipated a group of sober and pessimistic young people to be the outcome. I couldn't leave them this way.

I removed from my desk a looseleaf binder titled, "A Handbook for Teachers," produced by the school district. I asked the students if they were aware of the section entitled "Students' Rights." They were not, but indicated interest. So we began to investigate what essentially boiled down to "the role of the student in the decision-making process of the school district." The bell rang. Class was over.

Next day the students entered the classroom asking for the teachers' handbook and ignored me the entire period as they read and discussed its relevant contents. I wondered how many people would believe me if I told them that a group of "slow" students was, with great interest, involvement, and motivation, laboriously studying something as dull and dry as the teachers' handbook. They were reading selections from the state school code eagerly. The bell rang. Class was over.

This incident illustrates that we can often profitably begin with the students' questions, their interests and personal needs, and use subject matter accordingly. Reading emerges out of such questions, interests and discussion.

NEW BEGINNINGS

We need to be more daring in using resources. It's not that we shouldn't use texts, but we should use them differently. Don't *assign* a chapter. *Suggest* the text to help resolve a serious question—one the students think is serious. Of course, many texts can't answer serious questions and should serve only as a beginning. And many times, a text shouldn't be the beginning. The beginning might be a few days of just talking, a film, a field trip, or a guest speaker. I took high school psychology students to a mental institution for a full day of seeing and experiencing the first week of the term. The next day I asked if there was anything they wanted to know as a result of the visit. The rest of the term I answered their questions. And they read. We invited guests to class; we spent one or two days a week for many weeks in the library. I checked 50 to 100 books a week out of the library on the subject of interest for students to use in class and to take home. I surveyed daily, weekly, monthly, and quarterly publications for pertinent articles and made enough copies for half the students. I told them briefly about the article and *invited* them to take a copy if interested. About half the students would take copies, each time a different half.

I also had a deal with the librarian. Each Monday she had a cart ready with about 100 books on it. I'd push this to my room and Monday would be look-at-the-new-books day. About 10% of them would be checked out by the end of the day—not many, but over the year they'd add up. The result: lots of purposeful reading—purposeful from the students' point of view.

Another thing I've done is share interesting excerpts of whole books with my students. When I read *Black Like Me* I decided to share it with my students. One day I read just two paragraphs, enough to get them on the edges of their seats. Then, to their dismay, I closed the book. They pleaded with me to read more. I told them to get the book and read it themselves. The next day I saw dozens of copies in the class.

On another occasion I began a class by telling the students I wanted to read them a book. They needn't listen if they didn't find it interesting. I began reading *Anthem* by Ayn Rand. It took three days to read. During the first period I tape recorded as I read. During the other class periods I played the tape. When I finished reading the book, I asked them what they thought of it. We discussed it for only 15 or 20 minutes. A few days later I saw dozens of copies of Ayn Rand's books in students' hands. Not only *Anthem*, but also *We the Living, Fountainhead*, and *Atlas Shrugged*. The li-brarian wanted to know why I had assigned Ayn Rand's books without telling her. She had only one copy of each title, and over 50 students had signed up on the waiting lists for the books.

DON'T READ THIS!

A few years ago I had a student at Brigham Young University, a senior, who confessed to me he hated to read and had done little reading while in college. He told me this because I had announced at the beginning of class that no text was required. There would also be no reading assignments during the term; I would bring handout articles each class period, but the students need not take or read them if they did not wish to. Each class period I gave a sales pitch on the articles, which were related to the topic at hand. I knew that once students tried one of the articles, they'd try more. Of course I just happened to have 200 more in my office.

I noticed that the senior took none of the handouts. I began to tease him and bait him. I'd sometimes turn and tell him not to take a particular article because it would answer such-and-such a question or explain such-and-such an idea. Or I'd say, "You don't need to feel any obligation to take any of these handouts because I know you don't like to read." I'd also take books from my office library and "show and tell" the class about them. As they asked questions or brought up topics, I'd often refer them to a particular book as containing some excellent ideas and thinking regarding the topic. The student who "hated" to read would often smile at me and leave class without my handouts.

The day after the class ended, the student came to my office and said to me, "Okay, I've kept my word. I haven't read a thing. But now that the class is over will you give me copies of these articles? Also would you loan me two books that you mentioned in class?" I gave him the two dozen articles and loaned him the books. A week later he returned them. We sat and visited. He said he wanted to thank me. Because I hadn't "required" him to read, he hadn't had to resist me. By using reverse psychology, I had begun to stimulate his desire to read. I hadn't pushed him to read. I'd said, "don't read!" Even though I said it with a smile on my face, he still had begun to lose his desire to resist. Since reading the articles and books, he was hooked. He was sure he would be doing a lot more reading from now on.

Your students can't read, won't read? I've got a surprise for you. Reading can be made necessary to students and it can be made necessary naturally.

Reading Motivation through the Teacher-Parent Partnership

by Nicholas P. Criscuolo

Ask teachers what concerns them about reading and many will reply that their chief complaint is motivating children to read. Ask parents the same question and you'll get the same response. Motivation, attitudes toward reading—these are the terms and phrases that surface when a group of parents and teachers get together.

It's also often true that when children enter first grade, they come home the first day quite dejected. Why? Because they hadn't learned to read that day! They soon realize that learning to read is not an automatic process. Although some children learn to read easily, others experience difficulties, some all through their school careers.

Since it is the unmotivated, reluctant reader who concerns teachers and parents, this concern can be an excellent vehicle for forming a strong home-school partnership. This article will describe briefly ten effective ways parents and teachers can work together to motivate children to read.

1. Teachers can encourage parents to help their children select books to read independently by explaining the "Rule of Thumb" technique to them. Have the parent ask his/her child to open up a book and read a passage orally. Every time the child comes to an unknown word, instruct the child to hold up a finger of one hand. When the child comes to the thumb, chances are that the book is too difficult. This technique not only allows parents to help their children choose books they can read without frustration, but also stresses the importance of having children read for pleasure.

2. Teachers should be encouraged to provide time during the school day for children to read something of their own choice just for the fun of it. Whether it is an uninterrupted sustained silent reading period or not, time should be allocated during the school day for this activity. Parents can do the same. After the supper dishes are cleared away and the television set is turned off, parents should set aside a time period where everyone in the family reads—whether its a book, magazine or newspaper.

3. Parents are extremely interested in the academic achievement of their youngsters, therefore teachers should schedule conferences with parents periodically to discuss the progress their children are making. As part of this conference, teachers can supply book lists and suggestions for games which can be purchased locally and which not only reinforce reading skills but serve as motivational devices.

4. Parents often ask teachers what materials they can use with their children at home to motivate reading. The newspaper, which many families subscribe to, is an excellent learning resource which has something for everyone. Teachers can supply some home activities using the newspaper. Here are two examples. *Coupon Clippers:* Encourage your children to clip cents-off-coupons for the weekly shopping trip. The child can then use his/her skill of classification in categorizing the coupons, i.e., clothing, food, etc. *Vocabulary:* Encourage your children to pick a "Word For The Day" from the daily or weekly newspaper. This should be an unknown word and children should be encouraged to use the dictionary to look up word meanings to help increase vocabulary.

5. A parent once asked the late poet Robert Frost how she could motivate her children to read. His reply

was, "Surround them with so many books they stumble over them." Unfortunately, some homes do not have a good supply of books for children to read. This problem can be resolved by teachers and parents working together through PTAs to initiate Book Banks. Through the media, members of the community-at-large whose children are grown and who have books gathering dust on bookshelves at home can be asked to deposit appealing, usable children's books in Book Banks set up in various parts of the city. These books can be sorted and given to children to keep as part of their personal home libraries. The Book Bank project fosters the concept of pride of ownership, gets books into the home and encourages the reading habit.

6. In order to nurture the reading habit, it is crucial for teachers and parents to know the interests of their children. At the beginning of the year, teachers can devise and administer a simple Interest Inventory, or use the popular "Spaceflight Application For Reading" published by Continental Press. Since the teacher is also aware of the child's instructional reading level, he or she can consult a variety of booklists and recommend to parents several titles of books on the child's independent reading level which capitalize on those interests revealed by the Interest Inventory.

7. Most children, whether reluctant readers or not, have hobbies which can lead to reading. For example, one teacher set up a spot in the room called *Table Top Acres* at which were placed different varieties of plants along with literature on plant care. Children who want to learn about plants are motivated to read this literature. At home, whether their children's interests are cooking, making model airplanes or sporting events, parents should be encouraged to make appropriate literature available to nurture the formation of hobbies and lead into reading.

8. Just as we encourage children to eat a balanced diet, a balanced reading diet can also be encouraged. Teachers and parents often complain that children will read only mysteries or biographies. This is really not a major problem since at least they're reading! But it is

worthwhile for parents and teachers to work together to induce reluctant readers to diversify their reading. This can be accomplished easily both in school and at home by a simple device such as dividing a paper plate into various sections labeled "Mystery," "Sports," "Science Fiction," etc. Every time a child reads a book under a certain category, he/she can draw a design within that section. A child who has all designs in one area can be encouraged to "round out" the design by reading in other areas. Each child's design plate can be prominently displayed in the classroom and in the child's room at home.

9. The current emphasis on basic "survival" skills offers another effective way parents and teachers can help reluctant readers. As part of the instructional program, the teacher can secure materials such as store catalogs, job applications, menus, career booklets and driver's manuals to help students meet their personal needs for information and recreation. At home, members of the family can engage in such activities as checking clothing labels before purchase, planning a diet, and reading food labels for nutritional information. There are numerous home situations which lend themselves to reading that parents must be made aware of.

10. Teachers can spark reading through a variety of writing activities, especially those which involve their personal touch, such as notes and messages to students or instructions to those involved in independent projects. They can form Pen Pal Clubs where each child writes to a child in another school or area. Parents can encourage their children to write letters and thank you notes for birthday or holiday gifts.

Many articles have appeared in the literature offering tips and strategies on motivating children to read and often the home and school are considered separate units in this endeavor. But the home and school can work together through a variety of interrelated activities and, by reinforcing each other, add needed strength and support to attack the problem more effectively. It is this partnership which will ensure success.

Section III
Programs

The School Library—The Alpha and Omega of Your Elementary School Reading Program*

by Lea-Ruth C. Wilkens

THE PRINCIPAL INITIATES THE NEW PROGRAM

Yes, your school library (media center) can be the Alpha and Omega of your reading program and turn failures into successes if you, "Dear Principal," are daring enough to take the first enthusiastic step and let everyone around you know that the library is the place where reading connections are made and reading appetites are nurtured and nourished.

Yes, it is you, "Dear Principal," who makes the Alpha connection by volunteering to fill the reading or storyteller's chair in your library for at least one hour every week. You might call this hour a time of renewal. Renewal in the sense that you divest yourself of your garments of authority and, as if by magic wand, become the Pied Piper who leads children to the realization that reading and listening can be a very titillating experience. In reading to children, you, like the Pied Piper, take it upon yourself to charm children out of the confines of their texts into the wider world of reading found in the thousands of books available to them in their own school libraries.

Your second daring step then is to convince your teaching staff that you consider the library the heart of your reading program. In that sense, the library, like the heart, should pulsate new life into every classroom where reading is taught. For it is the library where gifted as well as reluctant and retarded readers can select from thousands of books and other materials that one specific item that will suit their particular reading needs.

READING READINESS AND THE SCHOOL LIBRARY

No child in your school is ever too young to be introduced to the magic place called the library. Kindergartners in particular need to be surrounded with books, books and more books if we expect them to develop voracious appetites for the printed word. All children need to be saturated daily with stories which will stimulate their imagination and keep their curiosities amply nourished. For instance, an appreciation and sense of language and word power can be cultivated very satisfactorily through the use of Mother Goose rhymes. The musical quality of these rhymes has rarely ever failed to tickle children's ears. Before long then, they will be eager participants who find great delight in letting even the more difficult words roll across their tongues easily and expertly.

Alphabet books, counting books, and concept books should not be overlooked as valuable tools to help children make that all important transition from thinking and perceiving only on the concrete level, but also on the more advance abstract level.

*"The School Library—The Alpha and Omega of Your Elementary School Reading Program" appeared in *Reading Horizons* (Fall 1979, pp. 55–59). It is reprinted with permission from the author and the publisher. Copyright © 1979 by *Reading Horizons*, Western Michigan University, Kalamazoo, MI.

Kindergarten children should also have the opportunity to take their first giant step of selecting their very own books to take to the classroom and then to their homes. By letting kindergarten children use their own books they can immediately be introduced to the basic prereading skills of caring for books, turning pages, looking from left to right, looking up and down, using picture clues, and even reading a few basic sight words.

For the kindergarten child there is no better place than the school library to make the Alpha connection that will lead to reading success.

THE SCHOOL LIBRARY AS THE CATALYST TO ASSURE READING SUCCESS FOR YOUR PRIMARY GRADES

Today's school library can also truly be the catalyst to spark the enthusiasm of your first grade readers. Most exciting among the hundreds of books and other materials which are available to first graders is a new series of books generally referred to as "I Can Read Books," or "Read Along Books." These books have been written especially for beginning readers who have been told so frequently by well meaning parents and grandparents that they would be able to read books once they entered first grade. Children, of course, more often than not, have interpreted this to mean, "I will be able to read a book at the end of my first school day." These easy to read books can nearly make this promise become reality because they were written using vocabulary which first graders either know already or want to learn very quickly. Many of the titles also reflect the interests which first graders have expressed over many years. Even though children live in the age of robots they still continue to ask for books which deal with ferocious dinosaurs, dogs, cats, slow moving turtles, and even minute tadpoles which sooner or later grow into not so minute bullfrogs. The attractive illustrations which cover part of each page, furthermore, enhance the exciting plots and help the beginning readers in realizing their reading goals through the additional help of picture clues. Even the overall format of these books has been planned carefully so as to closely resemble the type of book a more advanced reader might take home. All of these qualities appear to the beginning readers who have waited so long to be "grownup" when it comes to reading.

In schools where the basal readers may not be taken home by children the easy to read book can truly be the lifeline which will keep the reading program between school and home intact.

Students who were avid library users as first graders usually become even more avid library users as second graders. Children at this age level also have that urgent desire to become more self-sufficient in how and what type of material they want to select. Because they are so full of that unquenchable thirst for knowing more about the world around them, they are even willing to learn how to use the card catalog in order to find the books and materials which might answer their questions. Although they come to the library to read on their own, they still like to be read to and experience the world of make-believe and high adventure.

Second graders, like any other grade, also have that special need to find corners within the library where they can read and browse either alone or with trusted friends who might share in the fun and laughter which a book might bring. It is the kind of experience which seldom emerges in a structured classroom where only formal reading practices are allowed which are not always conducive to making the beginning reader understand that reading can also be an exhilarating experience.

Many librarians have also introduced puppets in their libraries. These puppets serve as listeners for those students who find reading difficult and need additional practice outside the classroom. A puppet sitting next to these special readers can instill that extra confidence needed by some of these children so that they may better survive in the very competitive classroom environment. "Frieda" as one of these puppets might be called, has unending confidence in the troubled reader, and if you believe in magic, you might be able to overhear Frieda whispering in the children's ears, "Don't worry, I won't tell anyone, just try it again."

Another item in the library that has always attracted the attention of second graders is the "rare" bookshelf. These books might rightfully be called rare because they have been written and illustrated by fourth and fifth graders with that rare charm and humor with which only children are endowed at this stage of their lives.

For second graders the library is like a kaleidoscope which, when turned again and again, will continue to bring new reading adventures.

Ask third graders what they like best about a library and they will probably tell you that it is the place where the *Guinness Book of World Records* is kept. It is the place with the reference shelf where answers can be found to such pressing questions as: "Who ate the most worms at one time?" "Who has the largest ears?" "Who has the smallest feet?" Another very tempting place in the library is the listening station area where they can try out their mechanical skills and wind, roll and thread tapes, films, filmstrips and view and listen to materials which will enrich their textbook lessons and help them prepare for social studies reports.

The library can also be the mentor for teachers who need to encourage the shy child to become a more active participant in creative group activities. Wordless picture books, when looked at and talked about in a magic circle, usually have the power to entice even the quietest child to participate and come forth with welcome responses.

Third graders also consider a poetry learning center set up for them in the library a very special place they like to come to. Poems dealing with such current themes as wheels, monsters, skateboards, and wishes, have a very special drawing power. In fact, before long you will probably find your students not only eagerly reading poetry but actually writing their own Haiku, Diamante and Cinquain poetry. This, of course, means that another successful reading connection has been made between classroom and library.

TOWARDS READING INDEPENDENCE AT THE INTERMEDIATE GRADES THROUGH THE SCHOOL LIBRARY

For fourth and fifth graders the library functions as a place of self-discovery. For them the library becomes the Alpha connection between the reading requirements of the classroom and how these requirements may be applied in the world to which they return after school.

In their basal readers, for example, they might be introduced to a unit on newspaper writing and publishing. Follow-up and extension activities in most basal readers usually suggest that students read certain articles in a daily newspaper and then attempt to follow this up with their own headlines and/or writing an article which might be published in a classroom or school paper. The prime purpose of the assignment, of course, is to promote the habit of daily newspaper reading for both information and pleasure. While the classroom teacher might motivate children by having additional newspapers available in the classroom, it is in the library where students can pursue the topic in greater

depth through the use of an interest center set up for them. Such special items as galley proof, type, and makeup page, can usually be obtained from a local newspaper. A ''real life'' reporter might even be present at the center for a few hours to add that extra touch of reality to the project.

Other reading connections to the outside world can be made by asking community volunteers to come to the library so that they might share with students how reading and their particular professions are very much interrelated. For instance, volunteers with such diverse backgrounds as bicycle repairing, weather-forecasting, farming and truck driving might be a very challenging and worthwhile beginning.

Reading and civic responsibilities can be presented through the cooperation of the local League of Women Voters who might be invited to come to the library when local or national elections are imminent. The presentation of campaign issues in all likelihood will arouse not only fervent debates but also bring about more critical reading habits if the students are asked to carefully examine the campaign issues through the various media made available to them in the library.

For the intermediate grades the library can, without doubt, be the most important Alpha and Omega link towards the development of lifetime independent reading habits.

In schools where the library has been allowed to be an integral component of the reading program, reading suddenly stops being fundamental for teachers and students only, but rather becomes fundamental for everyone within the school and outside the school. The term fundamental in itself takes on new meaning and becomes ''FUN''damental. It is a special reading aura which permeates the entire school and can easily be detected by the positive attitudes that teachers and students exhibit both in their work and in the environment in which they work. ''Quiet' signs have been banished from the library. Bookshelves no longer look like soldiers parading for review, but rather like soldiers on active duty to the reader. There are no empty walls or drab spaces in these schools. Every corner has been utilized to display completed work or work still in progress. Every corner has been used to help all children make the all important Alpha and Omega connection to a successful lifetime reading program.

Sixth Graders Write about Reading Literature

by Lewis B. Smith

"I guess life is twice as fun if you're in two worlds—the book world and the real world."
—Sonya

"I now know when life in reality seems hard, life in books is sometimes harder."　　　　—Julie

"I only wish Anne Frank could see how many people have read her diary and how they felt."
—Debbie

"You can always tell who loves books because they never look bored."　　　　—April

Children become committed to volitional reading when they read the finest writing available to them—children's literature. My experience as a fourth grade teacher in a school that had no basal readers supports this assertion. This suburban Cleveland school community believed that children should learn to read by reading library books. Books of this kind corresponded most closely to what children should read when they left school, and the children developed into independent self-reliant readers. I tell my graduate students about the success of this reading program in producing students who like to read, read by choice, and read a great deal.

Lisa, a sixth grade teacher, was among those enrolled last summer in my graduate class on psycholinguistics and reading. She employed this approach to reading instruction in her classroom and sent me a packet of letters from her students in early winter. Their comments reveal an emerging conviction that volitional reading was becoming meaningful to them. A second group of letters written in early spring shows marvelous insights. The children express in their own words many

of the understandings teachers would be pleased to have for instructional goals in reading. Through personal experience and self-discovery most of Lisa's students had come to believe in reading.

With Lisa's suggestion a correspondence between her sixth grade students and their teacher's teacher began. Excerpts follow from Lisa's and her students' letters, plus my two letters in which I responded to each student's remarks.

LETTER EXCHANGE

From Lisa . . .

December 2
Enclosed are some letters from my sixth grade class. I thought you would enjoy them. I told them you were my teacher last summer and that you are a "book freak." They are doing great in their reading . . .

From the students . . .

Hi, my name is Terri and I'm a book freak too. Today, December 2, I'm reading *Ramona the Pest* just for my pleasure.
. . . Terri

I am a very slow reader and I want to be faster. My mom says the more I read the better I'll get . . . If the books are challenging and I keep reading those that are, will I get better?
. . . Jamie

We have got shelves and shelves of books at home, and my mom has read every one of them. She is worse at reading than I am. I suppose that's why I like reading so much.
. . . Bruce

I hate to say this, but I don't like books. My eyes are bad. I'm farsighted and have to wear glasses. I hate wearing them. Mrs. Small told us that you helped her. I might be a teacher when I get older.

... Vicky

I didn't like reading very much until I had Mrs. Small as my teacher. She taught me how to love books. I read a few that were interesting. I thought since those were so good there must be more interesting books.

... Suzie

To the class ...

I was so pleased to receive a letter from each of you. I am glad to know that you are reading. In this letter I will speak to each of you in response to your comments.

Several of you mentioned liking *Sounder*—the book that Mrs. Small has been reading aloud to you. Jane thought that its sadness was special. She's right. The memory of this book will remain with you for a long time. That's what great books do. *Sounder* was special to Tim too, because he owns hounds. Stacy noticed that the author didn't tell the names of the people and yet created very believable characters. A fine author can do that. Tina mentioned the emotional feelings stirred by the book because there was love for one another expressed. Terri realized the author was doing something to make the book special to her, though it was difficult to express in words.

Deena and several others mentioned that you didn't like reading before, but now you do. I think that's great! Mark mentioned that he didn't like his version of *Dan Boone*—it didn't pick up his interest, so he stopped reading. That's okay. You should read books you like, because if you spend too long trying to read one, you don't like, it may make you doubt reading itself. Jamie asked about this too—she gets discouraged because she reads so slowly. Her mom told her she would get better as she reads more. You do learn to read by reading, and by choosing books that interest you. The books should have some new words, but not so many that they discourage you.

Michael, you said you read at home. I like that! There's just not enough time for reading good books in school because there's so much other work to do also.

Vicky, I wear glasses too. They surely are a big help to me. I wouldn't be able to enjoy books without them.

Sonya, you mentioned how reading opens up that second world when you said "I guess life is twice as fun if you're in two worlds—the book world and the real world." You were a fine writer to express that idea so

well. Once we have discovered the gifts that good books hide inside their covers, we have something no one can ever take away from us.

Let me suggest two very interesting books for Mrs. Small to read aloud to you. *Julie of the Wolves* by Jean Craighead George is one. *The Bridge to Terabithia* by Katherine Paterson is the other. They are both the kind of books you'll always remember.

I would enjoy hearing from you again. This time instead of telling me the names of all the books you've read, tell me why one book seemed special to you. I'll get to know you better that way.

From Lisa ...

March 7

What a sensation your letter caused in class! That was so nice of you to respond personally to each of the students. You really caused some faces to beam. The fact that you place such importance on reading, and that you are a man is helping some of my non-reader boys. One of them is frustrated with the limitations of our school library. He has read every biography we have on mountain men and now he's consuming what's in our small public library. Two fellows who had been "problems"—one in behavior and attitude, and the other in lazy study habits—have become American Indian enthusiasts. Both sets of parents have noticed a marked improvement in general attitude. Some of my students are scurrying around finding the book titles you recommended.

Your respect for reading, and your placing it as an important part of life has influenced these youngsters. You make my task easier. I know it's time-consuming, but if you respond just once more this school year, I would appreciate it so much.

From the students ...

Thank you for the advice in finding a good book. We are all reading biographies and my favorite book is *The Diary of Anne Frank*. It was very moving and told how she had to die. I only wish she could see how many people have read her diary and how they felt. It is very sad indeed. . . . When I read a biography I feel like I'm the person in it. When they are hurt it is as if I am too. When Anne Frank died, I felt as if I had died too.

... Debbie

I am reading *Swiss Family Robinson*. Some of the words are awfully heavy. Thanks to Mrs. Small, our walking talking dictionary, I'm learning new words and understanding the book perfectly.

... Sonya

The Call of the Wild is the best book I've ever read because of the action, fighting and survival of Buck. The Indians thought he was an evil spirit and they called him the ghost dog. The primordial beast in Buck made the story one of the best I've ever read.

... Joe

Blubber is the kind of book I really enjoy the most because it gives me the feeling that I'm a character of the book.

... Terri

The biographies I'm reading and hearing in class are unlocking history before my eyes (ears actually). . . . I read *Into the Dream.* I hated it. It was phony. I was all excited in the middle and it dropped me like a rock. I have a wild imagination, but that's ridiculous.

... Sonya

Since I talked with you last I've gotten my report card. It was awful. I would rather not tell you what I got. But now I am improving. I have read more books in half of this quarter than in the last two.

... Mark

You can always tell who loves books because they never look bored.

... April

My favorite book was *Florence Nightingale* . . . I liked it because of the way she improved the hospitals and made them stay clean. Also she acted differently than any other person I've read about.   . . . Kristie

I think Beethoven's biography is fantastic. I can't believe such a small boy at his age could make up songs in his head.   . . . Stacy

(Debbie told me part of the plot in *Island of the Blue Dolphins,* then thoughtfully prompted,) . . . you'll have to read the book to find out if she lived or not!

... Debbie

I like it when the whole class reads together. I think that it makes me want to read more too.   . . . Jamie

I was deeply moved by this story (*The Hiding Place*). Different times during the story I had different feelings, sometimes good, sometimes hatred. I now know when life in reality seems hard, life in books is sometimes harder.   . . . Julie

To the class . . .

Thanks for writing to me again. I'm glad you're having such a good year together. There is no special order to my responses to each of you, so I'll just begin.

Steve, I'm glad to know you continue to feel *Crazy Horse* is your favorite book. You mentioned the qualities this time, the mixture of fear and happiness. Few of us are asked to prove ourselves as he needed to do. Many of us will never know how brave we are. People even differ on what they think bravery really means.

Jamie, you are right about Hans earning well deserved fame, and hanging in there even though he had hard times. It is interesting how much we respect that in others.

Mike, I'm sure I read one version of *Black Hawk* when I was a fourth grade teacher several years ago. Becoming a chief was a fine reward and also a great responsibility. I also taught sixth grade. In one of my classes we read about flatboating into the Ohio wilderness.

Kevin, I know you have found that reading can bring pleasure when you are on your fifth biography, and one book meant so much that you read it three times! I haven't read your favorite yet, but you make me want to because of what you have told me about it.

Stacy, don't feel awkward if biographies don't interest you. I only like some of them. I could suggest books better if I knew more about you. Some titles you might look at are *Charlie and the Chocolate Factory* by Dahl, *Half Magic* by Edgar, *Blackbriar* by Sleater, and *A Wrinkle in Time* by L'Engle. Be sure to ask the librarian for suggestions, then check the words in the book to see that you can handle most of them. Good luck!

Debbie, you described well the deep meaning that *The Diary of Anne Frank* has for many who read it. When the author of a biography helps us to feel like the person we are reading about, both we and the author are working together to recreate the life and events described. I think you would enjoy *The Endless Steppe* by Hautzig or *The Upstairs Room* by Reiss.

Joe, you really write a fine description of a book! If you wish, ask the librarian for other titles by Jack London—he has written more powerpacked books. Try Susan Cooper's *The Dark Is Rising,* and read *Julie of the Wolves* if Mrs. Small doesn't read it aloud to the class. It is about wolves and most of it is realistic. The author studied wolves extensively, and Eskimos too. Don't worry that the story is about a girl—she is really brave.

Tim, I'm glad you enjoyed *Sacajawea.* When I was in fifth or sixth grade we acted part of that experience. Since my name is Lewis, I got to play the part of Meriwether Lewis, and we gave the play for the other classrooms. There are quite a few books about frontiersmen for a fellow with interests like yours—check with your classmates. They have told me about some of them.

Tina, thank you for your letter. I'm pleased you're reading so much. For a variation on mysteries I'd recommend *The Dark Is Rising,* or *The Grey King.*

Jim, you thanked me for telling you about some favorite books. Did you get to look at either of them? You might like *Call It Courage* by Sperry, a real special book about courage of a different kind. Read the first two chapters before you decide.

Vicky, thanks for telling me about your reading. I haven't read the book you mentioned. Thanks for sharing it with me. If you want another great book about London, read the exciting story, *Master Cornhill*. It is about the plague and the great fire of London, and was written by Eloise McGraw.

Tina, you might enjoy Blume's *It's Not the End of the World*. Life can be hard, and some books help us be more ready for hard spots. Several good books do that.

Nicole, welcome to the class. Your classmates have been reading lots of biographies—they can suggest their favorites to you. Another suggestion is to check into some of the Newbery Award and Honor Books. Some of them may be too difficult, but many of them are great books.

I think most of you have learned that books can be your friends. Some of them help our imaginations when real life gets dull. Others help us better understand people or situations that are different from those with which we are familiar. Many of the better books bring us beauty and laughter. You meet some terrific people, some great animals, and you can have lots of excitement. As my seventy-year-old stepmother wrote me recently, "although I live alone, I will never be lonely because of the good books I get from the library."

Don't ever feel bashful about asking a librarian or bookstore person to help you select a book. That's what they are in business to do. And don't hesitate to say "I need something a little easier," or "I'd like something a little harder." No one can tell you that you ought to be reading something easier or harder. That's your business. But they can suggest good books to try that you don't know about. Don't try to force yourself to like a book. Instead, look for a book that gives you the feeling "I don't want to put this down," within the first few pages or a chapter. Many books are like that.

Best wishes in the days and years ahead. And, remember anytime you want some memorable experiences or new friends, a good book can provide them.

CONCLUSIONS

Following are some of the important discoveries of these sixth graders.

- If some books are good, there must be others that I'd like too.
- It's okay not to finish a book if I don't like it.
- There's not enough time in school to read so I'll read at home too.

- Kids who love to read don't look bored during reading time.
- Good biographies unlock history and make it real.
- Reading can be "just" for pleasure.
- If my parents read because they want to, I'll probably like reading too.
- Some books tell me about people who have talents far beyond my imagination.
- Books tell me how hard life was for others and what they did about it.
- One can be so absorbed in good books that he or she forgets to misbehave or to be lazy.
- I respect the acts of human and animal bravery and determination that I have read about in books.
- Books tell how others have solved difficult problems.
- I like it when someone is interested in why I enjoyed a book and I can tell them about it.
- Sometimes I feel hurt and sad for the person I'm reading about in a book.

Discoveries like these and a strengthened personal commitment to read ought to be our highest goals for reading. Classrooms at all levels can provide students with opportunities to make similar personal discoveries. If we wish to create the atmosphere in which this can occur, literature in the form of library books and fine paperbacks must win a place of importance in our classrooms and in our schools. With a planned emphasis on literature, children will believe that reading books is an important life choice they may make.

REFERENCES*

Armstrong, William H. *Sounder*. New York: Harper & Row, 1969.

Beckhard, Arthur. *Black Hawk*. New York: Responsive Environment, 1968.

Blume, Judy. *Blubber*. Scarsdale, NY: Bradbury, 1974.

Blume, Judy. *It's Not the End of the World*. Scarsdale, NY: Bradbury, 1972.

Cleary, Beverly. *Ramona the Pest*. New York: Morrow, 1968.

Cooper, Susan. *The Dark Is Rising*. New York: Atheneum, 1973.

Cooper, Susan. *The Grey King*. New York: Atheneum, 1975.

---

*Some of the bibliographic information was added by the editors.

Dahl, Roald. *Charlie and the Chocolate Factory*. New York: Bantam, 1977.

Eager, Edward. *Half Magic*. New York: Harcourt, Brace, Jovanovich, 1954.

Frank, Anne. *Anne Frank: The Diary of a Young Girl,* rev. ed., translated by B. M. Mooyart. Garden City, NY: Doubleday, 1967.

Garst, Shannon. *Crazy Horse*. Boston: Houghton Mifflin, 1950.

George, Jean. *Julie of the Wolves*. New York: Harper & Row, 1972.

Hautzig, Esther. *The Endless Steppe: Growing Up in Siberia*. New York: Crowell, 1968.

L'Engle, Madeleine. *A Wrinkle in Time*. New York: Dell Publishing, 1962.

London, Jack. *The Call of the Wild*. New York: E.P. Dutton, 1968.

McGraw, Eloise Jarvis. *Master Cornhill*. New York: Atheneum, 1973.

O'Dell, Scott. *Island of the Blue Dolphins*. Boston: Houghton Mifflin, 1960.

Paterson, Katherine. *Bridge to Terabithia*. New York: Crowell, 1977.

Riess, Johanna. *The Upstairs Room*. New York: Crowell, 1972.

Seibert, Jerry. *Sacajawea*. Boston: Houghton Mifflin, 1960.

Sleator, William. *Blackbriar*. New York: E.P. Dutton, 1972.

Sleator, William. *Into the Dream*. New York: E.P. Dutton, 1979.

Sperry, Armstron. *Call It Courage*. New York: Collier Books, 1973.

ten Boom, Corrie. *The Hiding Place*. New York: Bantam Paperbacks, 1971.

Wyss, Johann. *Swiss Family Robinson*. New York: Grosset & Dunlap, 1949.

The author expresses his appreciation to Mrs. Lisa A. N. Small and her sixth grade class in Post Falls, Idaho for their friendship and correspondence.

Management Systems in Secondary Reading Classrooms*

by Christine C. Smith, Carolyn Burch,
and Grace Warren

One outcome of federal, state or district funding of reading programs has been the development of a competency based curriculum with the inclusion of a classroom management system. This management system is the structure for the implementation of the goals, guidelines and behavioral objectives of the program. Each program with its management system is developed and written by teachers in consultation with school and/or district level cooperation.

The management system in use in the secondary reading classroom should also reflect the teacher's theoretical approach to the teaching of reading. The teacher needs to know what approaches are soundly based in research and how to go about selecting an approach which fits into his teaching style and methodology. The management system would then be a natural outgrowth of a well defined theoretical base. The system therefore would not be randomly selected from samples available and artificially implemented in the classroom.

The teacher's management system and the district's management system do not need to be mutually exclusive. The selection of structural components from each system can reflect the teacher's position and the district's position at the same time.

*"Management Systems in Secondary Reading Classrooms" appeared in *Reading Horizons* (Spring 1980, pp. 207–14). It is reprinted by permission of the authors and the publisher. Copyright © 1980 by *Reading Horizons,* Western Michigan University, Kalamazoo, MI.

A WHOLISTIC APPROACH

The purpose of this paper is to present a management system which reflects a wholistic (reading-language arts) approach to the teaching of reading. Only the management system and the wholistic approach will be discussed. The suggested materials for the teaching of reading both teacher made and commercially prepared which are listed on the sample contract are not discussed due to limited space. However the teachers in the program did use traditional reading materials in a carefully controlled wholistic approach in an innovative setting in the teaching of reading. They avoided assigning individual practice of a hierarchy of skills. The management system and wholistic approach was developed and implemented in an ethnically mixed urban junior high school over a period of four years.

Teachers and researchers who espouse the wholistic approach view reading as a unitary act. The act should not and cannot be subdivided into bits and pieces of a hierarchy of reading skills. Rather it incorporates the various natural linguistic systems of the reader into a wholistic interrelationship of the graphophonic, syntactic and semantic cues of graphic language.

Reading strategies should involve the students' natural internal tendencies to reconstruct meaning from the writer's written message. In performing this process the student utilizes his natural predicting, confirming and comprehending strategies. These strategies are utilized in listening, reading, writing, and oral language activities through cooperative teacher planning between the classroom and the reading laboratory situation.

Wholistic (reading-language arts) strategy lessons are then based on the diagnostic assessment of individual needs of the students. Diagnostic assessments include the *Reading Miscue Inventory,* criterion referenced tests, standardized reading tests, and informal diagnosis. Contracts and record keeping can then be devised for each individual student in the classroom and reading laboratory with compliance with any existing federal, state or district guidelines.

A WHOLISTIC MANAGEMENT SYSTEM

The following management system was implemented in a Title I reading/English program at Charles Maclay Junior High School in Los Angeles. The Title I program, involving five seventh and five eighth grade classes, focused on the wholistic approach. This approach was selected after careful assessment of the students' reading status which indicated a need to strengthen their graphophonic, syntactic, and semantic cue systems in all the language arts (reading, writing, oral language and listening). The management system became an integral part of the reading/English program for each Title I student.

The teachers agreed that a successful wholistic reading program must implement three goal areas. These goal areas would be personalized through the implementation of the affective and cognitive areas of growth. Three cognitive-affective goal areas were identified and developed to: (1) provide for reading, both for pleasure and information; (2) provide for personalized skill development in listening, reading comprehension, writing, and oral language; and (3) improve the students' attitudes toward themselves, each other, and the school.

In order to meet these goals efficiently, a complete management system was devised. The management system includes: (1) a reading/English classroom/reading lab rotation schedule, (2) reading lab contracts, (3) goals and objectives for lab and classroom, and (4) pupil profile charts.

Classroom/Reading Lab Rotation Schedule

The reading/English classroom and reading lab management system is based on a five-week rotation, see Chart 1. The reading/English classrooms, of approximately 30 students, are divided into two groups of equal size. The 15 students in Group I go to the reading lab four days during Week 1 and four days during Week 2. Friday of each week is spent with the entire class in the classroom. The students in Group II follow the same schedule of going to the lab during Weeks 3 and 4 while Group I remains in the classroom. During Week 5 all 30 students remain in the classroom. On the following Monday the rotation begins again with Group I. The lab is closed on Fridays to allow time for correcting stu-

	Week 1 & 2		Week 3 & 4		Week 5
CHART 1					
	M-Th	Fr	M-Th	Fr	M-Fr
Classroom A CGAI CGAII	CGAII	CGAI CGAII	CGAI	CGAI CGAII	CGAI CGAII
Classroom B CGBI CGBII	CGBII	CGBI CGBII	CGBI	CGBI CGBII	CGBI CGBII
Reading Laboratory	CGAI CGBI	Lab Closed	CGAII CGBII	Lab Closed	Lab closed for new contracts and Learning Center Production

CGA = Classroom Group A   CGB = Classroom Group B

dents' work and is closed during Week 5 to provide time for preparing new contracts and new learning stations.

CLASSROOM ORGANIZATION

On the days that the student remains in the classroom he/she works with approximately 14 other students, a teacher and a teaching assistant on individualized reading, skill development, vocabulary, spelling, reading comprehension, writing and any other special project the classroom teacher has devised. As previously stated, Friday is spent with the entire class in the classroom. This day can be used for unit testing, introduction of new material, review, group presentations, etc.

Record keeping of daily attendance, classroom grades, and reading level grades is the responsibility of the classroom teachers. The reading laboratory teacher gives her reading lab grades to the classroom teacher at the end of each 5-week period to be incorporated into the student's total grade.

This rotation system, Chart 2, offers the classroom teacher many options for managing the classroom. Some special advantages for the teacher and the student develop as a result of this management system.

1. The teacher may group students in various ways within one classroom.

2. The teacher can work with small groups of students giving her the opportunity to watch students work and to observe their thought process in operation. This enables the teacher to see mistakes in progress, thereby allowing her to make instant corrections.

3. The teacher plans her lessons for a two-week block of time which fits the time one group is in the lab. This lesson is repeated once again for Group II. By doing this, the teacher's preparation time is minimized.

4. The teacher has more time to deal with individual differences between students.

5. Student work can be immediately corrected for instant feedback.

6. Students have a choice of personalities. They don't have to work with the same person every day. The teacher and teaching assistant alternate working within the groups.

7. The student has a two week period of time to intensively work through a unit. This gives the slower student a better chance to advance at his own rate.

8. Students can read both for pleasure and for information during a concentrated period of time.

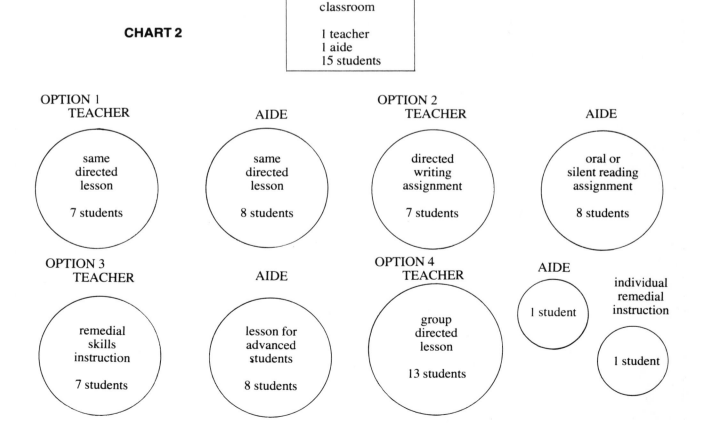

CHART 2

classroom

1 teacher
1 aide
15 students

OPTION 1
TEACHER — same directed lesson — 7 students
AIDE — same directed lesson — 8 students

OPTION 2
TEACHER — directed writing assignment — 7 students
AIDE — oral or silent reading assignment — 8 students

OPTION 3
TEACHER — remedial skills instruction — 7 students
AIDE — lesson for advanced students — 8 students

OPTION 4
TEACHER — group directed lesson — 13 students
AIDE — individual remedial instruction — 1 student — 1 student

Reading Lab Organization

Thirty students are in the lab at one time, approximately 15 seventh graders and 15 eighth graders. The responsibility for personalized skill development is with the lab teacher. In the lab, each student works on a personalized contract based on skill areas. Students are given their first contract based on the results of the *Stanford Diagnostic Reading Test*. Subsequent lab contracts are based on the student's achievement on the completed contract. Eighth grade students are given a contract based on work completed in seventh grade. The lab is staffed by the reading coordinator and two teaching assistants. Additional help is provided by ninth grade tutors.

The basic management tool in the lab is a student contract. Since the program's philosophy is wholistic in nature, each contract covers various skill areas incorporating listening, reading, writing and oral language activities. Student contracts are monitored and revised as students become more proficient. The materials covered in the contract are arranged in various learning centers so the students move around the lab from one center to another as directed on the contract. Correcting of work is done by the lab teacher and the teaching assistants and is done, as often as possible, as soon as the student completes the assignment.

The contract provides a detailed schedule of the student's work and progress over the two week period spent in the lab. Each contract (Chart 3) contains important information and instructions for the student, as well as for the teacher. The contract, as indicated by letter, provides:

CHART 3

Name_____ Contract #_____ Period #_____ Teacher_____

SKILLS TO BE LEARNED

7th Grade STATIONS	Main Idea	Word Attack Sentence Analysis	Comprehension	Creative Writing	Creative Expression	Survival Skills	Multicultural Listening	Prefixes Root Words	How did I do on each exercise? ********** Excellent Good, Fair Poor	Points Possible	Points Earned
Specific Skills	*		Book		Unit					20	
Reading Practice Program		*	Unit		Lesson						
Match Challenge Feedback Spark			*							10 20 30	
Newslab			*	Blue	Green						
Tell a Tale				*						100	
Word Pictures					*					50	
What's In a Label?		Do		Exercise		*				10 20	
Business Letters		Write			Letters *					20 40	
People Understanding People							*			10	
Nonsense Monsters								*		50	

A. A list of all skills covered on that contract
B. A list of learning stations
C. Instructions to the student about levels of difficulty and amount of work to be done
D. The order in which students should go from one station to the next
E. A self-evaluation column
F. A grading column

After the student completes the contract, the lab teacher and teaching assistants correct the student's work, give a grade to the contract, and give the grade to the classroom teacher who incorporates it with the classroom grades for report card grading purposes. (The classroom teacher is responsible for all official attendance taking and for all final grade recording.) A new contract is written for each rotation period.

Some special advantages exist in the contract system of organizing a reading lab and are as follows:

1. Students have an element of choice while following a structured contract. Each station can provide a selection of activities from which the student can choose.

2. Different learning styles can be accommodated in the same classroom. Students working at different stations can be using different approaches to learning.

3. Students can vary the order in which they finish their assignments. A student need not strictly follow the order of the contract, but can alternate one assignment with another.

4. The teacher using the contract has essentially made a lesson plan for all of the students which will cover a four-week period of time. This requires much concentrated planning at one point, but then frees the teacher for individual work with the students and gives her more time to plan future learning stations.

5. The various skill areas incorporated in teaching reading from a wholistic viewpoint can be presented to many students at various ability levels at the same time.

Goals and Objectives, Pupil Profile Chart

Since the reading program is wholistic and language arts based and incorporates both cognitive and affective areas of growth, the goals and objectives (skills) to be taught reflect this basic theoretical wholistic approach. These goals and objectives for the reading program are developed cooperatively between the classroom teacher and reading laboratory teacher. These lists of goals and objectives are a part of the overall daily planning of strategy lessons and the 5-week overview. Lesson plans for the classroom and the reading laboratory contract are devised and coordinated so that they complement each other.

In addition to the goals and objectives for the program, individual pupil profile charts are kept in the reading lab. All of the skills taught in the classroom and lab are recorded on the pupil profile chart, thus keeping a two-year progress report on each student.

CONCLUSION

There are advantages of incorporating the wholistic approach to teaching reading into a management system. This approach enables many students of many different abilities to study and become more proficient in the areas of listening, comprehension, writing and oral language. The students are better able to receive well-balanced reading instruction and will begin to see the reading process as a "whole." As they achieve success they begin to feel more positive toward themselves, each other and the school. While working as a united team which shares talents and skills, teachers in both the classroom and reading lab can successfully coordinate this wide spectrum of skills into a meaningful program.

REFERENCES

Goodman, Kenneth S., ed. Miscue analysis: applications to reading instruction. Urbana, IL: National Council of Teachers of English, 1973.

Page, William D., ed. Help for the reading teacher: new directions in research. Urbana, IL: National Council of Teachers of English, 1975.

A Recreational Reading Program for Disabled Readers: It Works!*

by Marilyn A. Colvin and Elton Stetson

Much has been written about the desirability of turning disabled readers on to reading. Replacing negative feelings and disinterest which disabled readers typically have toward books is one of the most difficult tasks of all. But when disabled readers report little or no encouragement from home the challenge becomes even greater. Recent research has shown three very important factors in developing interest in reading—all three factors within the home: (1) fathers who read to children; (2) mothers who read to children and; (3) the availability of easy reading material in the home.[1] When asked about reading habits and home involvement via the *Literature Preference Inventory*[2] disabled readers tutored at the University of Houston Diagnostic Learning Center reported very little home involvement (Colvin and Tomas, 1978). A tabulation of student responses concerning home reading habits revealed that 85% of the mothers and 95% of the fathers seldom or never read to them. The prospects of turning these readers on to books did not look bright. The following paragraphs detail the Recreational Reading Program (RRP) implemented at the Diagnostic Learning Center in order to meet this challenge.

GOALS

Turning kids on to reading is the primary goal of the RRP. This goal is based on the premise that children can read provided they are encouraged in a positive way to read materials that are within their capabilities or area of interest (Estes and Vaughn, 1973).

Because success or failure as a reader is often shaped more by the influence of the home than by the classroom teacher or materials used at school (Larrick, 1975), a second goal of the program is direct parental involvement. By using informal questioning techniques after their children have completed a book, parents become more intensely involved in the reading development of their youngsters. Parents also participate by receiving information concerning sources from which inexpensive books may be purchased to begin or expand a home library (Scholastic, 1978; Perfect School Plan, 1978).

A third goal of the program is to initiate lifetime reading habits. Initially, extrinsic rewards are provided to help overcome the reluctance disabled readers usually have toward pleasure reading. Ribbons and free books are awarded according to the RRP Rule Sheet (See Figure 1). The achievement of intrinsic motivation is realized as parents report continued positive effects of the RRP for youngsters after they leave the center.

PROCEDURES FOR IMPLEMENTATION

After a brief discussion of the program and rules, a Book Certificate inscribed with the child's name is displayed in the tutoring area. Along side the certificate a reward ribbon is displayed to illustrate to the child

FIGURE 1. Recreational Reading Program— Rule Sheet—distributed to students and parents during the first day of the recreational reading program.

RECREATIONAL READING PROGRAM (RRP)
Rule Sheet

1. READ ONE BOOK
   a. selected by the student
   b. paperback or hardback
   c. fiction or non-fiction
   d. subject of the book selected by the student
   e. newspapers and comic books do not count
   f. the book has never been read before

2. TALK TO AN ADULT ABOUT THE BOOK
   a. book should be read entirely
   b. no tests or book reports are required
      BUT
   c. the student must talk to an adult about the book (a parent, adult relative, or the teacher will do)
   d. the adult should interact informally with the student by asking questions such as;
      —Tell me about the book.
      —What else happened? *or* What happened next?
      —Who was your favorite character? Why?
      —What was the best part of the book?
      —Was there someone or something in the book you didn't like? Why?
      —Would you like to read your favorite part to me?
      —What did you learn from the book?

3. ADULT SIGNS CERTIFICATE OF READING EXPERIENCE (CORE)
   a. must be signed by adult who interacted with the student about the book
   b. adult could be mother, father, adult relative, teacher, or even a responsible adult sibling (high school or older)

4. TURN CERTIFICATE OF READING EXPERIENCE (CORE) IN TO THE TEACHER TO RECEIVE RIBBON
   a. certificate of reading experience required before ribbon can be awarded
   b. CORE forms are filed in student's work folder
   c. ribbons are displayed in the DLC until the end of the term

5. READ TEN BOOKS—RECEIVE ONE FREE BOOK
   a. book to be selected from the trade book library
   b. award label with the student's name is attached to the cover of the book
   c. read thirty books, receive three free books

6. BOOK CERTIFICATE AWARDED AT THE END OF THE TERM

what he will be working for. The last ten minutes of the typical sixty-minute tutoring period is used by the child to check out books from the center's trade book collection. Assisted by his tutor, the youngster selects one or more books on his independent reading level (Betts, 1957; Guszak, 1978; et al). A Certificate of Reading Experience (CORE) form helps keep track of books read and insures that books are being read (See Figure 2). Several of these forms are sent home with students on the first day of tutoring and must be signed and returned before ribbons are awarded.

Parents are also informed of the program through parent meetings conducted by the Center's staff. Parents are taught how to interact with their child when books have been completed. Emphasis is placed on informal sharing and parents are asked not to make the experience a grueling drill on facts and details but rather a pleasurable exchange of plot, character analysis, likes and dislikes. The RRP Rule Sheet and CORE forms identify the types of information questions to be asked.

Signed CORE forms are returned to the tutor who awards ribbons and displays them next to the Book Certificate. After ten books have been read, students earn a free book of their choice. An inscription, "Presented to John Doe for reading ten books, July 15, 1978," is added to the book's cover by the tutor. The Book Certificate and ribbons may be taken home on the final day of tutoring.

RESULTS

During the first summer school term of 1978, eighty-five students attended the center daily for remedial instruction in reading. During this four-week period an average of nine books per student were read— one student read twenty-six books. All participants received at least two ribbons and thirty-five students received at least one free book.

In order to get feedback from parents, an RRP questionnaire was used during the last week of tutoring.

FIGURE 2. Certificate of Reading Experience (CORE)—forms distributed to parent(s) to be completed when the student has completed a book and interacted properly with an adult.

CERTIFICATE OF READING EXPERIENCE
(CORE)

Name of Student_____

Name of Book_____

Author_____ Publisher_____

I, (parent, teacher, or other adult's name) _____ do solemnly certify by affixing my name to the line provided below that the above named student did indeed read the book described above and talked with me about the book, its main characters, what happened to the characters in the book, and told me whether or not he/she liked or disliked the book. This Certificate of Reading Experience, when presented to the teacher, entitles the student to receive one ribbon.

_____   _____
DATE   ADULT SIGNATURE

_____   _____
DATE   STUDENT SIGNATURE

When asked to rate the effects that the program had on changing their child's attitude towards reading, 33% reported that the program had a "dramatic" effect in a positive direction and 64% felt that the effects were "definitely positive." Only one parent reported no effect. In addition, all but one parent stated that they would continue a similar program at home after the tutoring session was over. When asked to comment on what they considered to be the most positive aspect of the RRP, the most frequently appearing parent statement was that the entire family felt the effects of the program and that communication among family members was enhanced. Many added that the program influenced them to read more as well.

Overcoming the negative feelings many disabled readers have toward reading is difficult but far from impossible as evidenced by the success of the RRP described above. With care devoted to involving parents and matching disabled readers with interesting as well as easy recreational reading material, turning on to reading is unquestionably possible. Try it! You'll be as convinced as we were.

REFERENCES

1. Sucher, Floyd. Address presented at the Greater Houston Area Reading Council, Houston, Texas, International Reading Association, March 1977.

2. Abrahamson, Richard, & Stetson, Elton. *Literature Preference Inventory*. A survey document administered to students attending the University of Houston Diagnostic Learning Center, 1977.

BIBLIOGRAPHY

Betts, E. A. Foundations of reading instruction. New York: The American Book Company, 1957.

Colvin, Marilyn A., & Tomas, Douglas A. A summer reading methods practicum that works. *Epistle*, 1978, *5*, 1–4.

Estes, Thomas H., & Vaughn, Jr., Joseph. Reading interest and comprehension implications. *Reading Teacher*, 1973, November, 149–153.

Guszak, Frank. Diagnostic reading instruction in the elementary school (2nd Edition). New York: Harper & Row, 1978.

Larrick, Nancy. Home influence on early reading. *Today's Education*, 1975, 64, 77.

ADDITIONAL RESOURCES

Perfect School Plan (a program sponsored by the school to encourage parents to purchase books and magazines—points are awarded to the schools for purchase of equipment), Box 866, Philadelphia, Pennsylvania 19105.

Scholastic Book Services, 908 Sylvan Avenue, Englewood Cliffs, New Jersey 07632.

Tell Your Story with a Reading Fair

by Concetta Wilson-Gebhardt
and Corlea S. Plowman

In a large community there can be many obstacles to overcome before a school system can be certain accurate descriptions of its services, programs and goals are reaching the public. Sending notes home to parents is not enough.

To inform and gain the support of the people of Newport News, Virginia, the school division has taken its reading program into the community. For the past four years, Newport News Public Schools have held a reading fair at one of the area's largest shopping malls. The reading fair allows the school division to obtain maximum coverage and reach the 140,000 community members. Although it requires additional work for teachers and administrators, the reading fair has been so successful that the staff is already planning the fourth annual event.

Pulling all the division's reading resources together for one public presentation requires organization and attention to detail. The experience of the Newport News Reading Fair might assist others wishing to take their reading story to the public.

There's no big tent and the lions are caged in book bindings, but the Reading Fair has all the excitement of a Barnum and Bailey production. For maximum visibility, we chose to hold our fair in a two-story shopping mall. With ample parking, it is accessible to all of our citizens, and because it is enclosed, no rain dates are necessary. A Saturday is great for teacher, parent, student and shopper participation. Setting hours from 10 a.m. to 6 p.m. maximizes the fair's impact and allows the "ringmaster and performers" to enjoy the event.

Once the location has been selected, the following steps will help outline the work ahead for a successful fair. First, contact the mall marketing director. (This person will be important to the success of the fair, so begin to establish a good rapport.) Set a date for the fair at least five to six months in advance and establish the times for set-up and take-down.

Ask about advertising the fair in the mall a week in advance of the event. This might involve large signs. (Sometimes the mall management may be willing to paint and pay for the signs if you prove you can attract a large crowd the first year or two.)

It is important to obtain a drawing of the mall floor plan with the locations of electrical outlets. This helps when assigning displays that may need electrical power. Be sure to check the type of wall plugs. (Will you need adaptors, such as pig-tail plugs? Will the mall furnish extension cords?) All electrical cords should be taped down with duct tape. It is a good idea to assign someone to be in charge of anything "borrowed" from the mall or you may end up paying for missing equipment.

If you plan to have children performing, determine what platforms and microphones the mall has. Arrange to bring your own equipment if they don't have any. Make sure you are aware of the rules and regulations the mall enforces.

Recheck your arrangements with the mall manager several months before the fair. Contact that office again several weeks prior to the fair to make certain that all equipment will be ready.

THE MAIN EVENT

Involve everyone in your school system who is associated with reading—reading consultants, psychologists, volunteers, librarians, etc. By all means, invite outside agencies who also work with school children—city libraries, Literacy Council, PTA, volunteer groups, and local colleges if they work with your system.

Several people should be assigned to coordinate the displays. For our fair, each school has one side of an A-frame display to show anything they want. Coordinators check each frame to make certain that the work is in the correct form for public display.

The coordinator should be on hand the evening before the fair and early the morning of the fair to make certain that things are in place.

A table, tablecloth (or paper skirt) and sign are needed for each participating group. These tables should be colorful and attractive. Make the signs uniform and large enough for passing shoppers to read. If the school system allows you to use its large tables, arrangements must be made for delivery and pick-up.

SPECIAL EVENTS

Invite local dignitaries to participate. We invite school board members and administrators, state representatives, city council members, local TV personalities (especially those on children's shows), etc. to read to children during the day. To organize this, have someone write letters inviting these people to participate. Send requests several months in advance because these people have busy schedules (don't forget to call or send reminders a week before the fair). Set a time schedule giving each reader about 30 minutes and send copies of the schedule to those dignitaries who accept. Have a few standby readers just in case an invited guest can't make it at the last minute. Have a wide variety of books on hand for the readers to select.

We include a local storyteller. We have had the president of the Regional League of Storytellers. You may have a librarian or parent who could tell children's stories. For seating you will need a chair for the reader and a rug for the children. A small microphone and speaker are handy. (Each year a store in the mall has furnished us with a comfortable chair and a rug. A sign near the reading area acknowledges this fact.) We also put a sign next to the chair that reads "Our Reader Is" and the name.

Involve teachers and their students. Ask teachers to have their classes perform at the fair. Oral reading, skits, drama and mime are all effective. Assign someone to be in charge of the performance part of the program and coordinate this with the readers' schedule to eliminate possible competition for an audience.

Another successful activity is showing films of favorite children's stories. To do this, rope off a "movie area" away from the readers and performers. Use rear-screen-projection equipment (eliminates need for darkness) and about 15–20 folding chairs. Assign someone to select short movies and reserve films in advance. Obtain necessary equipment and schedule projectionists for continuous showing. These films need to be short enough that parents can view them with children and young children don't lose interest.

Bring reading to life with people dressed as their favorite book characters. Local college students who work with our reading program dressed as Bo-Peep, the Cat in the Hat, Little Jack Horner and other characters. They walked throughout the mall telling people about the fair, bookstore discounts and giveaways.

BONUS FEATURES

Ask bookstores in the mall to give a 10% discount on any book or material in the store during the day of the fair. You should contact the bookstore manager months in advance to make arrangements. Print cards (business card size) which are used to receive the discount and give them away at your displays. The card should include the school division's name, Reading Fair date (good only for the day of the fair), names of participating bookstores and "10% discount." We also list the Newport News Reading Council, which cosponsored our fair. You might ask some volunteers to help bag merchandise at the bookstores. The merchants appreciate the extra hands. The discount cards are collected at the cash register. If you run out of cards, pick up the cards at the bookstores and recirculate them.

Another bonus is our giveaways—bookmarks, balloons and information. We gave away handmade bookmarks as well as bookmarks from The Children's Book Council. We printed handouts with reading activities of all varieties for teachers and parents, and distributed balloons with a reading motif printed on them. Helium and string are needed for the balloons. Be sure to assign someone to coordinate giveaways and to order all materials in advance.

ANNOUNCING THE EVENT

Posters announcing the fair should be printed and displayed around the city—in all schools, local stores, city buildings, etc. Several days before the fair send home with every student a flyer announcing the event. Press releases sent to newspapers and radio and television stations also help advertise the big occasion.

Photographs of the fair will be useful later in slide-tape presentations and brochures.

FOLLOW-UP

Keep a notebook containing information about things which were purchased, memos and letters written, names and addresses of everyone who participated in any way. This notebook will be extremely helpful when you plan the next fair.

Have your staff dismantle the displays within the hours you and the manager have set. The displays may be lost or damaged if you do not take care of this.

Assign everyone to the cleanup crew. Be a thoughtful guest of the mall and leave your areas cleaner then when you came.

See the mall manager immediately after the close of the fair to discuss the fair's success. You can use the information, particularly their visitor count for the day, to evaluate and plan for your next fair.

Write thank you notes to everyone who participated or helped in any way. In the notes mention the specific function(s) performed by each participant.

The Reading Fair has proven to be an exciting event for teachers, students, parents and the community. The rewards—community involvement and awareness—make the Reading Fair well worth the time and effort.

Parents and Students Communicate through Literature

by Pat Scales

Too many parents express interest only when they disapprove of books their children read. Few of them ever communicate a genuine excitement for the reading experience. This fact is evidenced by the increasing number of censorship cases and declining reading scores among the students in this nation.

Educators are certainly alert to these existing problems, but the numerous strategies for solving them can be questioned. Public demand has forced a greater emphasis on the teaching of reading skills; therefore, books are used primarily in the instructional process. Yet, opportunities to stress recreational reading are often neglected because of individual and societal biases, teacher accountability, and a limited knowledge of the literature.

Because today's parents have less time to spend with their children, reading is not a top priority in many homes. Even parents who have enjoyed books with their preschoolers tend to lose interest once their children begin to read independently.

ADULT FEARS

When children reach their "middle years" and individual interests emerge and reading choices change, parents who appear uninterested in their children's reading habits may only be frightened because of their restricted knowledge of the literature. They remember from their own childhood ardently collecting the Hardy Boys, Nancy Drew, and the Bobbsey Twins, and though such series have survived the years, children today are more interested in reading the humor of Beverly Clearly, the mysteries of John Bellairs, and the fantasies of Lloyd Alexander.

Adults confront an even greater misunderstanding concerning the reading needs of young people in contemporary adolescent literature. *Don't Slam the Door When You Go, Early Disorder, Killing Mr. Griffin, Are You In the House Alone?, About David,* and *Love Is a Missing Person* are titles which evoke attention from both adults and young adults. Unfortunately, while the young are reading and discussing the books, adults are only reading the blurbs. They read words such as rape, pregnancy, abortion, drugs, suicide, and divorce, and they rush to schools, libraries, and bookstores to complain about the literature their children are reading.

They want to protect their children from the mores of a changing society and teach them that all of their hopes and dreams will be fulfilled. Mothers have fond memories of Betty Cavanna's *Going On Sixteen* and Maureen Daly's *Seventeenth Summer,* and they expect their daughters to flock to these titles with the same enthusiasm. Dads are anxious to share *The Deerslayer, Huckleberry Finn,* and *Robinson Crusoe,* while grandparents proudly present leather-bound editions of Alcott, Brontë, and Dickens.

Attempts to share such reading experiences are certainly based on good intentions, but today's youth are more concerned with the pressures of their own world. They are willing to discuss the books they are reading, but they want to talk with open-minded adults who share their concerns.

THE ISSUES

The issues are crucial. Are current reading programs in public schools effective for developing positive attitudes toward reading? Are educators concerned enough for the reading direction of the young to initiate programs that will stress the values of adolescent literature to parents?

Such issues have been carefully evaluated by the faculty and staff at Greenville Middle School (Greenville, SC), and the results have produced new designs in reading curriculum. The reading program at this middle school is centered upon one premise—that the more students read, the better they read. Germane to this philosophy is the belief that faculty, students and parents must share reading experiences in order to achieve the ultimate goal of developing good, life-long reading habits.

THE PROGRAM

Once a month parents are invited to the school's library for a special program planned by the librarian. Entitled "Communicate Through Literature," the four-year-old program has three primary objectives: (1) to develop positive communication between parents and their children through the use of literature; (2) to encourage a better relationship between the school and community by involving the parents in the school program; and (3) to create a supportive atmosphere for intellectual freedom by providing parents with the opportunity to study and analyze young adult literature.

Discussions concerning reading interest of young adults, special needs of the reluctant reader, and the importance of reading together as a family challenge parents to make reading a major part of their home environment. Efforts are made to identify and analyze the unique personal needs of the adolescent, and parents are encouraged to relate these needs to their children's reading choices.

The meetings are held at 10:00 a.m. while students and teachers proceed with their library activities. Parents see the library at maximum use, and students are fascinated by their parents' discussions. Library cards are issued to parents, and they are urged to use the library collection at any time. Immediately following the monthly meeting, they browse among the shelves and seek reading suggestions from observing students. Between meetings, many parents send messages requesting certain titles, and students provide the necessary courier service.

PARENT RESPONSE

Various feelings for the literature have surfaced. Parents who were once troubled by their childrens' request for "a sad book" now realize that such emotions and moods are common and necessary to the maturing process. They are beginning to relate a child's need for escapist literature to an adult's desire to view soap operas. Parents who initially viewed with guarded interest books dealing with such social issues as drug abuse, child abuse, alcoholism, divorce, and teenage pregnancies now realize that a desire to read about such subjects is not necessarily an indication that the reader is unhappy with his or her own life or engaged in wrong-doings. It is, however, an indication of natural curiosity to know and understand the conflicts which surround and threaten his/her world.

Several parental perceptions of the literature have evoked concern. One mother who noted the negative portrayal of parents in many of the young adult novels commented, "I certainly hope that my son doesn't view me this way. He probably does. Maybe I should think about this." Another mother expressed an extreme dislike for the "open endings" so common to contemporary literature. Upon discussing the issue with an eighth grader, she was surprised when the girl responded, "I like to supply my own endings. That way I can make it as happy or sad as I want." Though this mother accepts the idea that such endings provide the reader with an opportunity to think creatively and critically, she still prefers the comfort of the definite ending of the "happily ever after" novel.

Most of the adults do not share their childrens' interest in science fiction, but will readily read and discuss realistic fiction. They are not especially fond of the "thriller" or the didactic novel, but find a refreshing enjoyment in humor. They like historical fiction and short stories, but are bored with the superficial "series" novel.

CONTROVERSY MINIMAL

Books which have been banned or questioned in many public and school libraries are openly discussed in these parent meetings. Each person's views are valued and a mutual respect for individual opinions has developed among the group. The school has experienced no problems with censorship, and the majority of the parents have accepted "such books" with overt enthusiasm. As one mother stated, "I would rather my daughter read *Forever* at home and discuss it with me than snicker over isolated passages with her friends at a slumber party.''

One usually conservative parent became so thrilled with Judy Blume's *Deenie* that she chose to express her approval to the librarian in writing.

> ''Thanks for asking me to read *Deenie*, otherwise I might not have taken the time . . . I find it honest and true to the world of the adolescent . . . I prefer its answers to mine! I hope my daughter will read it soon. She is very interested now that she knows I've had the privilege.''

A father has expressed disbelief that anyone could question *The Cay*. ''It's such an important book. I'm happy that my son wants to read it a third time.''

A consistent number of parents have become actively involved and have alternately been willing to share the program with others. Parents from other middle schools have asked if they could join the group, and local community clubs have requested that the program be shared with them. Public librarians have willingly participated in the monthly meetings, and the P.T.A. has endorsed the school's entire reader guidance program by occasionally providing financial support.

Future plans include inviting participation from parents of children who attend the five ''feeder'' elementary schools. This invitation will amplify the current program by providing parents the opportunity to identify with the school's reading program before their children face the difficult transition to middle school.

IMPROVEMENTS NEEDED

The faculty of Greenville Middle School is aware of several problems with the existing program. Because of the meeting time, participation is now limited to non-working parents. There are plans, however, to expand the program to include night meetings. These meetings should solicit more involvement and open lines of communication to a larger percentage of the school community.

Informing parents of meeting dates is perhaps the most major problem. Because there is no budget for postage, students are asked to deliver announcements of meetings. Unfortunately, many of the notices are found on school buses or tucked away in lockers.

This problem is currently being evaluated by the parents and improvements are being planned for next year.

REWARDS

The rewards of the program are numerous. Adults and students are reading together, parents have grown sensitive to the reading needs and interests of middle schoolers, and faculty members feel encouraged by the students' excitement for books. The school administration enjoys the positive reactions expressed by the parents, and local bookstores and public library branches indicate that the entire school community has acquired a zealous taste for young adult literature.

Reading can become a fad, or it can be as dreaded as a mathematics exam. Libraries can become as popular as the local teen hangout, or they can be as quiet as the football stadium on a Monday morning. Parents and teachers can become involved in the reading experience of young adults, or they can take a passive attitude and risk a unique opportunity to communicate with one another.

Reading is a fad at Greenville Middle School, and the library is the most popular place in the building. But, most importantly, parents are involved in the reading experiences of their young adults. The enthusiasm for this involvement is best expressed in the following comment by seventh grader Kim Headley: ''If I read a good book, I'll ask my mom to read it. The books may help her see how I feel.'' Feelings are the basis for communication. Through literature parents and students are communicating!

Section IV
Activities

Developing Creativity through the Reading Program

by Charles E. Martin, Bonnie Cramond, and Tammy Safter

Teachers want to provide interesting and challenging programs of study for gifted children, but creating special programs is not always feasible in an already crowded schedule. An ideal situation would be to develop activities for the average student that at the same time challenge the gifted readers.

That is not so difficult as it may at first seem. Renzulli (1977) noted that many of the needs of the gifted student are similar to those of the average student, despite the fact that gifted learners usually possess advanced language skills which predispose them to rapid growth in academics—especially reading. This overlapping of students' needs is particularly true in creative comprehension—the ability to use information, obtained while reading, in new and unusual ways. In addition, the very nature of responding creatively to what is read allows for the open endedness and flexibility essential for an activity to be applicable to a range of students.

The following five strategies, which take advantage of the common need for instruction in creative comprehension and of the nature of the task, are techniques which regular classroom teachers can use with most children in their rooms.

SCAMPER

Torrance (1965) stated that the objective of the teacher in developing creative readers is to get the students to do something with what they read, either during or after reading. One method teachers have used is questioning. However, writing questions to elicit creative responses is not easy. Eberle (1972) used a method called SCAMPER to provide a set of guidelines for writing creative questions.

The letters in SCAMPER stand for the type of creative responses elicited when asking questions. The examples shown below are a result of applying this technique to reading *Little Red Riding Hood*.

Example

S Substitute:	What do you think would have happened if there had been an elephant in Granny's bed instead of a wolf?
C Combine:	How do you think the story may have changed if the Wolf had the same personality as Granny?
A Adapt:	How do you think the Wolf would adapt his plan if the Hunter had walked in with Little Red Riding Hood?
M Modify:	How can you rewrite the story to save the Wolf?
Magnify:	How would the story be changed if Little Red Riding Hood had been larger than the Wolf?
P Put to Use:	How could Little Red Riding Hood have used her hood to help her?
E Eliminate:	Rewrite the story without the Hunter.
R Rearrange:	What would have happened if Little Red Riding Hood had arrived at her Granny's house before the Wolf arrived?
Reverse:	Rewrite the story placing the Wolf in Little Red Riding Hood's character and Little Red Riding Hood in the Wolf's.

Teachers can use children's responses to these questions to lead into writing language experience stories. Children can share their answers and stories and discuss how events in the story led them to their conclusions. By taking advantage of reading, discussion, and writing, SCAMPER provides an excellent method for integrating all the language arts.

CREATIVE DRAMATICS

An alternative to simple questioning which also combines several of the language arts is creative dramatics. In this activity, children act out events in stories they read. The skits may duplicate the action or be more creative versions of their own interpretation. The dramas may place story characters in a different setting. For example: "What would happen to Robin Hood if, instead of Sherwood Forest, he lived in modern day California?"

In the early grades, puppetry is an excellent method for beginning creative dramatics. Children who are shy take part readily when allowed to "let the puppet do the acting." They can make their own puppets, design a puppet theater, and perform plays for their own class or others. If other classes are involved, advertisements and billboards may be constructed to promote the upcoming play.

Creative dramatics has numerous advantages over answering questions after reading. When responding to questions, it is difficult for children to display the same depth of understanding that is possible through acting. Also, questions draw attention to small portions of what is read, rather than to the story as a whole (Jett-Simpson, 1978). To dramatize, children must view the entire story, consider the interrelationships of characters and events, and interpret the characters' actions. With this information, they create a new reality in the form of a play and share their interpretation with classmates.

CREATIVE PROBLEM SOLVING

The first two activities help students produce creative responses to what they read. The third strategy, creative problem solving (CPS), carries this process one step further. The goal of CPS is to develop students who can read to discover problems and then creatively find workable solutions.

Torrance (1979) outlined five steps for the technique:

1. Fact finding: Reading to get information.
2. Problem finding: Deciding what is the real problem. It is not always what it appears to be at first glance.
3. Idea finding: Brainstorming possible solutions to the problem. Evaluation of ideas does not take place at this step. Wild ideas and novel solutions should be encouraged.
4. Solution finding: Deciding from all possible solutions which is best. Two ideas might be combined to form a best solution.
5. Acceptance finding: Selling the solution. Though a solution may be "found," others must be convinced of its value.

The activity starts by having students read the beginning of a story. The teacher stops the children at a point where a question or decision looms. For example, the teacher asks, "How can Terry get money to buy Mother a present?" The children then decide what is the real problem. They may decide that the problem is thinking of a job for a seven year old.

The children are then asked to think of as many possible jobs as they can for Terry. After brainstorming a list of possible jobs and writing them on the chalkboard, the students evaluate the solutions. They are evaluated according to criteria developed by the students: "If you were Terry, what are some of the things you would consider when choosing from these jobs?"

Once a job is selected, the teacher asks the students to decide how Terry would find such a job. Children would finally read the remainder of the story and compare their solution with the author's solution.

CPS might be conducted with a whole class when they are first learning the procedure. After students are familiar with the process, they may work in smaller groups. The groups' varied solutions can be compared before reading the author's solution. Which did they like best? Children can also rewrite stories using their ideas.

AMBIGUOUS STORIES

Brainstorming skills practiced in the solution finding stage of CPS may prove useful in the fourth strategy, ambiguous stories. This strategy calls for the teacher to present stories with intriguing situations which can be interpreted in many different ways, as in the following:

It was late and getting dark when I came to the house. Everything was quiet. All I could hear was the sound of my feet. Nothing else was moving. It was like I was the only person alive.

Suddenly, I saw something move behind the trees. I looked again but didn't see a thing. Was I imagining things?

No one could blame me for what was happening. I knew they would but if they were in my place they would have done the same thing. My friends would stand by me. I hoped they would.

I couldn't wait any longer. I had to be brave. Looking back at the full moon just over the trees, I went to the door and knocked.

Teachers should begin by telling their students that they are going to read a story in which they will have to use their imaginations. While reading, they should try to think of as many explanations as they can for what is happening. They should try to make their explanations fit the events of the story. Children may then share their interpretations with the entire class or in smaller groups, explaining why they made certain decisions. Other questions that are useful with ambiguous stories include: What would be good titles for the story? What could have caused what happened in the story? What questions could you ask to help you decide what the story is about? What might happen next?

Students should be encouraged to interpret the stories in as many ways as possible. As with CPS, stories can be rewritten according to favorite interpretations. Children can also practice writing their own ambiguous stories to share.

Teachers can create ambiguous stories of their own or use parts of stories that are already written. If they choose to write their own, several points should be kept in mind. The passage should tell a story, yet leave much to the reader's imagination. The details that are included should grab the reader's interest and elicit vivid images. Finally, the ending of the story should be open for the reader to fantasize.

To use stories that are already written, the teacher should seek passages with the characteristics described above. These points usually occur just before an exciting event. They are the build-ups authors create, the tensions that peak just before an important moment. In some cases entire stories may be used. (An excellent example for use with older students is "The Lottery," by Shirley Jackson; all but the last few paragraphs, that reveal the meaning of the lottery, can be read before questioning the students.) In other cases only part of the story might be used.

BRANCHED ENDINGS

The final activity to be discussed is branched endings. The objective is to create many possible story endings from the same beginning. Students are placed into small groups (four to eight children per group is best). They then read, or the teacher reads to them, the beginning of a short story that places its characters in a dilemma with two possible choices. Half of the group members select one of the choices and form a subgroup while the remaining members take the other choice.

The two subgroups discuss independently what they feel will happen next as a result of their decision to resolve the dilemma. One member of each subgroup acts as scribe and records their continuation of the story. This part of the story is ended by creating a new dilemma for the character to resolve in one of two ways.

The groups continue the process, dividing in half at each dilemma, or branch, until each child is writing alone. At this point the child writes an ending to the story.

The following is an example of the beginning of a branched story:

Tommy got on the bus. When it started he almost fell. It felt like someone pushed him or reached in his pocket. To make sure, he felt inside his coat. Something was there. A note. "Who put it there?" he thought. He opened it. It said: GET OFF AT THIS STOP.

The bus stopped and people began to get off. "Did the note writer get off?" Tommy said to himself. He looked up and saw an old man watching him. "What did he want?" Tommy wondered.

He looked outside the bus and saw a small old woman standing. "What was she waiting for?" he wondered. Is she waiting for me? Does she need help?" WHAT DOES TOMMY DO? DOES HE GET OFF THE BUS OR STAY ON IT? WHAT HAPPENS NEXT?

Having completed the process, students will have as many endings as they had members in the groups. The group can reassemble and see what others wrote and why they made certain choices. The group's work can be compiled to form a complete story whose readers will have to make decisions at each dilemma. Depending on their choice, readers will be directed to certain pages to continue reading, where they will soon have to make another choice. This continues until readers reach one of the endings. They may then go back in the story to explore where other decisions would have led them.

As with ambiguous stories, teachers have the option of creating their own story beginnings or using ones that are already written. In writing a story, beginning teachers should try to capture the readers' interest with immediate action. The situation should then quickly come to a point where a decision must be made by a character.

This occurs quite frequently in basal reader selections. A story can be read to the point where a decision must be made. Branching can begin from there. Most children's stories also contain points where characters must make decisions. Does Jack go up the beanstalk? Does Charlie in *Charlie and the Chocolate Factory* (Dahl, 1964) spend his last money on more chocolate candy?

APPLICABILITY

The strategies described attempt to increase the creative comprehension ability of every student. The degree to which these activities are applicable depends on their adaptation to individual classrooms. Flexibility is the key. Less able students may be placed in groups with better readers for some of the activities, especially those that require writing. Teachers may also read the stories to these students rather than have them read independently. For younger children, strategies may be modified to become language experience activities.

Finally, these creative comprehension activities are of particular importance to gifted learners. The gifted are our problem solvers and creative thinkers of the future. The development of their skills cannot be left to chance in an area like reading which will play an important role in their academic and professional lives. It is only through direct instruction in creative comprehension that these skills can be developed and reading used to its fullest potential.

REFERENCES

Dahl, Roald. *Charlie and the Chocolate Factory*. New York, N.Y.: Alfred A. Knopf, 1964.

Eberle, Robert F. "Developing Imagination through SCAMPER," *Journal of Creative Behavior,* vol. 6 (Fall 1972), pp. 192–203.

Jackson, Shirley. "The Lottery." In *Insight and Outlook*, edited by Murray Rockowitz, pp. 213–25. New York, N.Y.: Globe Book, 1970.

Jett-Simpson, Mary. "Reading Comprehension through Creative Dramatics." In *Using Literature in the Elementary Classroom,* edited by John W. Stewig and Sam L. Sebesta, pp. 63–71. Urbana, Ill.: National Council of Teachers of English, 1978.

Renzulli, Joseph S. *The Enrichment Triad Model: A Guide for Developing Defensible Programs for the Gifted and Talented.* Mansfield Center, Conn.: Creative Learning Press, 1977.

Torrance, E. Paul. "Creative Problem-Solving." Unpublished manuscript, University of Georgia, Athens, 1979.

Torrance, E. Paul. *Gifted Children in the Classroom*. New York, N.Y.: Macmillan, 1965.

Humor as a Motivational and Remedial Technique

by Clyde G. Colwell

For the student experiencing motivational or remedial problems in reading and language arts, humor as a learning strategy is often overlooked. The rationale for this approach is multifaceted, but readily understandable. Consider the following points.

- Young people have a sense of humor that is constantly curbed by reading and language art skills activities, which are normally quite dry.
- A large segment of students who encounter problems in reading and language arts have been labeled emotionally disturbed or learning disabled, and some come from unpleasant home environments. Rather than ease their burdens, unfriendly school climates (lack of peer acceptance and failing grades) may compound their problems. Subjecting such students to 12 years of compulsory education in a hostile environment may be tantamount to subjecting them to compulsory failure. Humor provides an outlet to ease the problem and motivate the student.
- We read and hear about the benefits of integrating the language arts and the value of actively involving students. Activities that include humor often do both.

Here are 12 specific suggestions (by no means an inclusive list) for making humor an integral part of the reading/language arts curriculum.

1. What's my line? Take a photograph from a newspaper or magazine (examples: strange facial expressions, baby photographs, animal photographs, unusual buildings) and add a one-line humorous caption. For a learning center activity, provide two or three completed examples. Then insert 5–10 pictures that need captions.

2. Advertisements we'd like to see! Place full-page magazine ads on one inside half of a manila folder. On the other inside half, include the same ad with the slogan(s) cut off. The student then invents a more humorous slogan. (Favorite targets: cigarette ads, detergents, nonprescription drugs.)

3. Can you top this? Take an existing single-frame cartoon (comic or political) and see if students can invent a more humorous caption. (Good source: "Wizard of Id.") Variation of the same activity: Don't show students the original caption until they have attempted one of their own.

4. Dear Penny: Provide the student with one or several letters from a newspaper column that offers advice on personal problems. Include typical problems that affect the age group you teach. Have the student compose a humorous reply. You may wish to use the best ones in a school newspaper or classroom bulletin board.

5. This pun's the one. Learning center activity: Define "pun" and give several examples. Then give the student (in writing) some contrived situations. Ask the student to reply to the situation with a pun. For example: What might a grocery customer say if a dozen eggs fell from the shelf and landed on her? Reply #1: The yolk's on me. Reply #2: That's not eggsactly funny!

6. The laugh center. Provide reading centers where students can read a humorous magazine, story, or book. Change selections every two weeks. Depending on their age and reading skills, they can start with simple humor (Mad Magazine, Crazy, Cracked) and gradually try more sophisticated humor (Langston Hughes, Bret Harte, Mark Twain).

7. Prime time TV (parody). Have the students work in small groups to compose a script for a scene from a popular television show. Then let them rehearse (possibly tape record) and eventually present the scene to the rest of the class or several classes.

8. Make me laugh. The student keeps a diary (for two weeks to a month) of favorite jokes from TV, magazines, peers. Once it is assembled, the student either presents jokes to the class as a monolog or has another class member come forward to act as listener. The second class member tries to maintain a straight face for two minutes while the other tells the jokes.

9. Talking picture (more advanced creative skill). The student uses an instant photo camera, then adds captions to humorous photographs.

(a) The student photographs humorous road signs, storefront signs, or marquees.

(b) Outside of school, various class members or others offer humorous poses. The student adds captions.

(c) The student can develop a series of related sequential photographs into a full, humorous story by adding words. This can be a group project that leads to a student booklet.

10. Teacher's turn. Take 5 to 10 minutes at least once a week to read something humorous to the class. The sources of material are unlimited. Examples: humorous item from the newspaper, five to six puns from a book of puns, a few pages from a humorous book.

11. Test anxiety. To dispel any test anxiety students may have, place one humorous item on the test. For example:

(a) Directions: five points will be given for spelling your name correctly.

(b) Multiple-choice: How did you feel as you took this test?

_____ A. Upset

_____ B. Anxious

_____ C. Nervous

_____ D. All of the above

(c) Multiple-choice: How long did you spend studying for this test?

_____ A. More than 5 minutes, but less than an hour

_____ B. More than 1 hour, but less than 2 hours

_____ C. More than 2 hours

_____ D. None of the above

12. The play's the thing. Have the student try to recall a humorous incident that happened in or out of school. The student lists the characters and writes the incident as a dialog. When appropriate, this can be acted out. As with the language experience approach,* the student is writing directly from personal experiences.

The number of outlets for creative humor is sizeable. Some activites can lead to student presentations, student booklets, and classroom bulletin boards. Others may be appropriate for the school newspaper or auditorium presentations.

Almost all of the activities described promote active student involvement in the language arts—thinking, reading, listening, speaking, and writing. Humorous activites may enable a student with a sense of humor to experience success, the best motivator of all.

---

*Editors' Note: Language experience is an approach to learning to read in which the student's own words are written down and used as materials of instruction for reading, writing, spelling, speaking, and listening.

Reinforcing Remedial Readers through Art Activities

by Deborah R. Jansson and
Theresa A. Schillereff

Remedial readers often display a lack of interest in reading which many authorities consider to be the result of repeated failure. For example, Fernald (1943) believes this lack of interest is the product of negative conditioning, and suggests that all remedial work begin with a reconditioning process that focuses on the child's accomplishments.

Reconditioning for success may be achieved in part with activities that center on the child rather than the teacher. Child-centered activities tend to be more meaningful and motivating, and therefore more likely to yield success for struggling readers.

Any form of creative art is an especially good child-centered activity. Art is adaptable to any classroom situation and to learning centers. Most importantly, the finished art product, which may be shared, enhances self-esteem.

RATIONALE

The use of art activities in this reading and language arts program is supported by a basic rationale.

Bookbinder (1975) argues for the use of art in teaching all the communication skills. He states that historically art has been used to communicate ideas, and that art is a means of communication in young children that closely parallels the development of verbal expression. Both Bookbinder and Gillingham and Stillman (1960) point out that the alphabet was based on picture writing. According to Bookbinder (1975),

One can also conclude that in education today the interrelationship of these means of expression should be kept in mind so that we may better serve the needs of enriching any one means (reading) by the use of the other related means (the arts).

Because literacy is not highly developed in young children, art can become their means of expression. Cohen and Gainer (1977) consider this expression to be a cognitive experience:

Art provides a key for understanding children's ideas and concepts. Perhaps more significantly, it enables children themselves to make tangible contacts with their own ideas and so better understand themselves.

Art activities may also aid the development of fine and gross motor coordination as well as provide for sensory satisfaction (Lamme and Kane 1976). Specifically, most art activities involve the visual, auditory, kinesthetic and tactile modes. This multisensory approach is fundamental to many reading and remedial reading programs in use today (for example, Fernald's, Spalding and Spalding's, and Gillingham and Stillman's).

ART IN ACTION

There are many simple art activities that don't require great amounts of space, materials or time. Following are short descriptions of those that can be used for teaching reading and for reinforcing related skills.

Grapho-linguistic method. Motivation is often high when children construct their own reading materials. This is the basis for the "grapho-linguistic" method (Platt 1977) in which the child begins formal reading instruction by drawing simple pictures. The teacher then helps the child label parts of the drawing. As Platt states:

> The crucial discovery these children made is that not only does everything have a name and a sound-image, but also everything has a written-image.

As the children learn basic vocabulary words and as labeling becomes spontaneous, modifiers and articles are introduced. Word phrases, and then sentences, continue to be added to the children's drawings until, at their request, lined paper and pencils are introduced. Platt added that the children experienced no difficulty in learning to write, perhaps because that skill had been introduced as a meaningful art form rather than an abstract concept.

Art and picture books. With Tana Hobban's picture book *Look Again!* (1971) children view a portion of a photograph through a small window in an overlay page. They guess what the picture is before turning the page. Both Donham and Icken (1977) and Larrick (1976) suggest using *Look Again!* to encourage creative writing. Donham and Icken use construction paper folded in half. A small hole is cut in the paper, revealing a part of the child's drawing. In Larrick's method the student draws a picture or cuts a photograph from a magazine and writes an accompanying description. Younger students may describe their "Look Again!" orally.

Donham and Icken also provide a list of 25 picture storybooks with related art activities. Larrick includes a list of 20 wordless picture books that may be used to teach reading and writing.

For appeal to elementary students, Lamme and Kane (1976) recommend 20 books whose illustrations are done in collage. They cite Ezra Jack Keats and Leo Lionni as particularly appealing. Again, after constructing collage pictures, students are encouraged to describe them in writing or orally for their classmates. Additionally, Lamme and Kane suggest collage for developing fine muscle coordination (handling scissors) and for providing gross motor exercise (tearing and pasting) and sensory satisfaction (textural differences).

Teaching concepts and words. Art activities are helpful in teaching specific concepts or words to slow learners (Nathanson, Cynamon and Lehaman 1976).

Comprehension of the concept "snow," for example, is taught via activities that include small group discussion, sensory stimulation, creative dramatics and audiovisual aids. After the preliminary work, the children make up simple sentences about the topic, orally. Then sentences are written on their drawings, which are displayed throughout the room. Children can combine several simple sentences to form poems. This activity not only helps the exceptional child to learn to spell a specific word but aids in making word associations.

Karstadt (1976) describes 16 art related and manipulative experiences for the teaching of reading and writing. A few include: forming clay snakes into words, painting words, and pasting stenciled letters into words. Karstadt's activities would be well suited to the learning center, with materials for each activity kept in shoe boxes.

Interdisciplinary approach. An interesting interdisciplinary approach to art, music and remedial reading has been presented by Mathias and Fanyo (1977), intended to give meaning and motivation to reading. Children read directions for the day's project, work on the project referring to the directions, and follow up their work with written summaries.

The teacher can use this approach to develop integrated lesson plans. A Halloween unit, for instance, might include developing songs, creating a Halloween ghost tree and pictures, writing recipes for a party, and reading Halloween stories. Mathias and Fanyo draw parallels in the areas of art, music and reading; for example, musical tones were related to color tones and sound blending.

Comic books. Remedial readers especially enjoy comic books. Sosnowski (1975) suggests cartoon making for teaching skimming techniques, remembering key ideas, and comprehension. After they've read an assignment, students develop questions and illustrate them in a cartoon format, working either in groups or individually. Sosnowski cites other advantages of the cartoon format, such as providing a guideline for study and encouraging concise explanation.

Creative art activities need not be restricted to remedial readers. However, we believe the creative art experience to be particularly appropriate for children who are having difficulty in reading and language arts programs.

What is necessary in providing a child-centered environment which integrates art with reading and language arts? Simply a willingness on the part of the teacher to allow the child to assume some responsibility for his/her learning. In other words, the teacher provides motivational materials, simple directions, individual help when appropriate, and time to share the finished art product. An appealing feature of the art experience is that no extensive training is necessary—you simply provide the opportunity to learn.

REFERENCES

Bookbinder, Jack. ''Art and Reading.'' *Language Arts,* vol. 52, no. 6 (September 1975), pp. 783–85, 796.

Cohen, Elaine Pear and Ruth Straus Gainer. ''Art as Communication with Children.'' *Childhood Education*, vol. 53, no. 4 (February 1977), pp. 199–201.

Donham, Jean and Mary L. Icken. ''Reading to Write: An Approach to Composition Using Picture Books.'' *Language Arts,* vol. 54, no. 5 (May 1977), pp. 555–58.

Fernald, Grace. *Remedial Techniques in Basic School Subjects.* New York, N.Y.: McGraw-Hill, 1943.

Gillingham, Anna and Bessie W. Stillman. *Remedial Training for Children with Specific Disability in Reading.* Cambridge, Mass.: Editors Publishing Service, Inc., 1960.

Hoban, Tana. *Look Again!* New York, N.Y.: Macmillan, 1971.

Karstadt, Roberta. ''Tracing and Writing Activities for Teaching Reading.'' *The Reading Teacher,* vol. 30, no. 3 (December 1976), pp. 297–98.

Lamme, Linda Leonard and Frances Kane. ''Children, Books, and Collage.'' *Language Arts,* vol. 53, no. 8 (November/December 1976), pp. 902–05.

Larrick, Nancy. ''Wordless Picture Books and the Teaching of Reading.'' *The Reading Teacher,* vol. 29, no. 8 (May 1976), pp. 743–46.

Mathias, Sandra L. Ess and Mary Massa Fanyo. ''Blending Reading Instruction with Music and Art.'' *The Reading Teacher,* vol. 30, no. 5 (February 1977), pp. 497–500.

Nathanson, David E., Amy Cynamon and Katharine K. Lehaman. ''Creative Writing for Exceptional Children.'' *Teaching Exceptional Children,* vol. 8, no. 2 (Winter 1976), pp. 87–91.

Platt, Penny. ''Grapho-linguistics: Children's Drawings in Relation to Reading and Writing Skills.'' *The Reading Teacher,* vol. 31, no. 3 (December 1977), pp. 262–68.

Sosnowski, Frank W. ''Report Making the Cartoon Way.'' *Grade Teacher,* vol. 92, no. 7 (March 1975), pp. 75–77.

Spalding, Romalda Bishop and Walter T. Spalding. *The Writing Road to Reading.* New York, N.Y.: William Morrow, 1969.

RBIs: Reading/Baseball Ideas*

by Naomi K. Skriloff

A friend called me unexpectedly one fall day and said, "I have two tickets for the World Series. Come join me!" It had been a long time since I was a young student living in Brooklyn and following baseball, so I was a bit unprepared for the changes. Whoever heard of a relief pitcher being driven out to the mound in a car? But one alteration in America's favorite pastime particularly held my attention—the electronic scoreboard and line-up announcement board. As I watched these visual technological devices flash words and symbols on and off, it occurred to me that baseball has numerous elements related to reading skills—from syllabication ("Reg-gie") to vowel sounds ("plaaay ball"), blends practice ("strike!") and slang ("awwrigght!").

By the next spring, when baseball fever was rising among my upper-grade students, I had devised a wide variety of reading activities based on a baseball theme. I hoped these would help my students with their continuous struggle to interpret the arbitrary symbols and letters that make up words. As it turned out, they not only honed their skills in the process, but also had a lot of fun. The interest level can stay high from the appearance of the first baseball card right through summer (when you may want to play summer reviews with parents) and into the fall when World Series mania takes over the country.

PLAY BALL!

1. *Library skills.* To research the history of the game, we went to the library and learned how to "break the library's code." We found that the "Arts and Play" section is the 700s and that 796 is the number for baseball books. The students also discovered how to look over a table of contents to preview a book. With this skill they were able to separate books on the history of the game from those on rules, for example. (For some of the books my students used, see the list at the end of this article.)

2. *Organizing skills.* Based on their library research, the students made chronological outlines on the history of baseball. They also learned how to organize paragraphs and use different styles. For example, for the topic sentence, "Baseball and softball are alike," they added other sentences to support the comparison. They did the same thing with a topic sentence on contrasts, such as "Baseball and football are very different."

3. *Sequence.* From the information on their outlines, I scrambled the subheadings and had the students arrange them in their proper order. I also took sentences from some of the resources, scrambled them and had students arrange them in the proper sequence according to the way events occurred.

4. *Visual skills.* I collected pictures depicting a variety of baseball actions, pasted them on cardboard and inserted cartoon-type balloons. By looking at a picture, a student had to figure out what was going on and then write appropriate dialog in the balloon.

As a variation of this activity, I asked the students to look at the pictures and then answer simple questions on the action. For example:

"The players around first base can be described as (1) asleep, (2) afraid, (3) excited."

"The coach with his arm around the pitcher is (1) trying to hurt him, (2) trying to encourage him."

*Reprinted from *Teacher,* April 1980. Copyright © 1980 by Macmillan Professional Magazines. Used by permission of the Instructor Publications, Inc.

"Player No. 5 is the (1) catcher, (2) coach, (3) left fielder."

A second variation consisted of giving each student or a group duplicates of the pictures and having them write down all the details they could see. Then they compared notes with other students or groups.

5. *Listening comprehension and direction-following.* I made up mimeographed sheets with various pictures relating to baseball. Then I asked students to follow directions such as these:

"Put an 'x' next to the bat."

"Place a line above the mitt."

"Make a circle at the bottom of the uniform."

"Circle the symbol which, placed next to a player's name on the ballpark board, indicates he's at bat."

"Draw a line on the top of the box that shows the umpire making the 'out' sign."

"Underline the box showing what the player who is at home plate uses."

6. *Vocabulary.* We did a number of baseball-related activities to expand students' vocabularies. One was to look for words with multiple meanings in the reading selections. Examples are: *fans, play, base, game* and *pitcher.* Vocabulary games included variations of bingo using baseball vocabulary and *Pronoun Pinch-Hitter* (Developmental Learning Materials) in which students make pronouns pinch hit for nouns.

I made baseball-word flash cards to build up speed in word recognition. For the same purpose I devised a "baseball player" tachistoscope using a picture pasted to cardboard of a player at bat. Next to the bat was a slit for a sliding card containing such words as *single, strike, double, foul, triple, home run, walk, ball, pop* and *fly.* I also used the cards and the tachistoscope to reinforce our phonetic and spelling-rule lessons. Using "y" as a vowel (*fly*) is an example.

A favorite vocabulary activity was a simple "Batter Up" crossword puzzle using only baseball lingo. After my students had done the one I devised, they made some of their own to challenge classmates.

7. *Word analysis.* By compiling lists of baseball players' names and running them off on mimeographed sheets, I was able to help students reinforce a variety of phonetic reading skills. For example, I asked them to find the blends (*Bl*air), irregular double vowels (P*au*l), words within a name (*Will*ie) or syllables (*Reg-gie*).

As a variation, I had the children rewrite the players' names in syllables on the back of baseball trading cards.

To give students further practice with the phonetics they'd been working on, I prepared groups of cut-apart words—compounds and words divided into syllables. The cut-out syllables and word parts were mixed up and the children reassembled them.

8. *The five w's.* To help students reinforce their understanding of *who, what, where, why,* and *when,* I asked them to select the appropriate word for the following sentences:

I saw the game *at Yankee Stadium.* (why, where)

We saw the game *yesterday.* (when, what)

The pitcher was retired *because he gave up too many hits.* (who, why)

The bats and balls are in the dugout. (why, what)

Did you meet *the coach*? (who, when)

9. *Context clues.* To improve the students' ability to use context clues, I constructed a cloze activity. From passages in several baseball books my students had used as references, I deleted every fifth word, except the proper nouns, and substituted a blank space as long as the omitted word. I left the first and last sentences intact. Then, the students filled in what they thought were the correct words. To check their work, they referred back to the books.

10. *Finding the main idea.* To help students take this first step in understanding what they read, I took paragraphs from a number of baseball resources and had them underline the sentence that stated the main idea. I also devised several other activities to reinforce this skill. For example, I gave the students untitled selections and asked them to put on their own titles; I had them match paragraphs with topic labels I wrote myself; I had them match simple two- or three-line paragraphs with specific baseball pictures.

As an enrichment activity, I asked each student to bring in a copy of the local newspaper and turn to the sports section. Each student took his or her turn acting out one of the stories while classmates skimmed the section to find the correct item. They also used the newspaper to keep up with current activities and team records, a good motivation for reading.

11. *Comprehension.* I wrote specific factual comprehension questions based on the resources we had available. For example: "What date and against what club did Reggie Jackson hit three World Series homers?" I also asked students to analyze copies of certain selections and decide whether statements were fact or opinion. They underlined facts in red and opinions in blue. A short article, "Strike Out Little League" by Robin Roberts (*Newsweek*, July 21, 1975), contained a good mixture of facts and opinions. For example, the youngsters saw how the use of the word *monster* for the Little League stated the author's opinion.

EXTRA INNINGS

To put their skills and baseball knowledge to good use, I had students write stories based on their own experiences with the game—playing or watching. This exercise was fun for the kids and stretched their thinking and language skills more than simply writing reports would have. For example, Artie wrote:

"Once, I was a little boy. I watched baseball on TV so much, I wanted to be a baseball man.

Now I'm so good I'm on the Little League team, and I'm getting better and better.

I play baseball in the Rockland Valley Little League. I play well there."

Little did I think when I accepted my friend's invitation to the World Series that I'd become so involved with the sport. I may even take my students out to the ballpark this spring to kick off another season of baseball and reading.

BOOKS ABOUT BASEBALL

The Baseball Life of Johnny Bench [Scholastic, New York, 1974] and *The Baseball Life of Mickey Mantle* by John Devaney (Scholastic) [New York, 1969]

Baseball Players Do Amazing Things by Mel Cebulash (Random House) [New York, 1973]

Behind the Plate: Three Great Catchers by Guernsey Van Riper (Garrard) [Scarsdale, New York, 1973]

Great Baseball Pitchers by Jim Brosnan (Major League Baseball Library, No. 6, Random House) [New York, 1965]

Jackie Robinson of the Brooklyn Dodgers by Milton Shapiro (Archway) [New York, 1973]

Reading

READING REMEMBRANCES

Too often in the rush to cover the curriculum, we miss the magic of the moment when a child discovers ''I can read!'' You can help capture some of that magic by having children start their own personal reading tapes—as soon as they can read a page or two.

Provide each child with a blank tape on which to record short readings throughout the year. (Whether the tapes are brought in from home or purchased by the school will have to be settled at the outset.) Although taping these short readings should not be too time consuming, you may be able to enlist the aid of parents to get all the students on tape as often as possible.

At the end of the year, each tape may be taken home as satisfying proof of reading progress (and perhaps to be added to the following year). The tapes are a great motivator for beginning readers, as well as a later reminder of those first magical ''I can read'' moments.
Idea by: Magdelina Smigulec, Mt. Clemens, Mich.

FILE 13

Letters, wedding and party invitations, cereal box panels, coupons, utility bills, washing instruction labels—all of these things have one important feature in common: they're all *readable*. As such, they represent a valuable resource for any reading program.

To give students the opportunity to practice their reading skills on real-life materials, begin by collecting a wide assortment of these ubiquitous readables. Along with the items mentioned above, there are: menus, tickets from sports or theater events, stamps, absentee voting ballots, bus and train schedules, as well as pages from comic books, catalogs, dictionaries, telephone directories, driver's manuals, calendars (the list is endless).

Mount each item on an 8½-by-11-inch sheet of tagboard and prepare questions and/or activities for each based on the skills you wish to reinforce—vocabulary, phonics, reading for detail, sequencing, etc. Laminate the sheets, put them in order according to difficulty, number them, and then place them in a file box labeled ''File 13'' (the pet name, in some circles, for the wastebasket).

Students can be encouraged to contribute to File 13, and to prepare their own questions or activities for the items they bring in. With or without student contributions, File 13 is sure to be a popular and productive addition to your reading program.
Idea by: Patricia Harris, Fairborn, Ohio

CRAZY CONNECTIONS

If your students tend to read their new vocabulary words, look up the definitions, pass tests on the words and then draw a blank the next time the words appear in a story, you may have a situation that calls for ''crazy connections.''

One of the keys to memorization is association. If kids can form vivid connections between the vocabulary words they need to remember and images, objects or people they're not likely to forget, the words may be easier to recall.

The next time you want to introduce new vocabulary to your reading group, invite the group to devise some offbeat connections for each new word—the stranger the connection the better. For example, students might connect the word *carrion* with *buzzard*, a carrion consumer, and use the double letters in each word as a visual reminder. *Frantic* might be connected with *crazy*, which in turn might be connected to wild-and-crazy Steve Martin, who then becomes wild-and-frantic Steve Martin—rendering the word *frantic* utterly unforgettable.

Besides helping to fix new vocabulary in mind, crazy connections make word building an entertaining activity in itself.

Idea by: Debra Martin, Portage Middle School, North Canton, Ohio.

FOCUS ON SPORTS

Sports is a subject that can provoke the interest of even the most reluctant readers. Here are some suggestions for using sports to enrich your reading program.

- Collect articles about sports events and personalities from newspapers and magazines; locate books and how-to manuals on the topic of sports. Set up a sports reading center for no-strings-attached browsing.
- Cut stories from sports magazines, mount them on paper, add comprehension questions, and staple the pages into manila folders. Display the folders as reading kits.
- Mount high-action sports photos in folders for students to use as the basis for ''what's happening'' paragraphs or stories.
- Invite small groups of students to brainstorm and then write up lists of sports trivia questions for other groups to read and answer.
- Tape-record radio broadcasts of sports events to use at listening stations. Follow up each broadcast with questions, or ask students to write short sports-page accounts of the action.
- Establish a school version of ''Sporting News.'' Assign each interested student a ''sports beat''—basketball, hockey, gymnastics. The student responsible for a particular beat regularly attends and writes up the event for news publication.
- Invite sports-related personalities (players, reporters, commentators, authors of sports books) to the classroom for discussion and interview sessions. (Both pre- and post-interview reading/search will be in order here.)

You can also take advantage of the spin-off opportunities presented in a sports-focus reading program. Research into sports history, a study of bones and muscles, an investigation of modern-day sports as compared to ancient sports—these and other areas for further reading exploration come to mind.

Students who seem to be in a reading slump may just need some new reading options to get them out of it.

Idea by: John Noel, Visalia, Calif.

RECYCLING FOR RECALL

For children with short memories for sight words, repetition in various contexts is the remedy. The following activities present a recycling process to help youngsters absorb new sight vocabulary. To get under way, you'll need to write the words on colored cards—one word to a card, a different color for each child in the group.

- **Cycle 1.** Gather the children together and have them bring their word cards. Each child in turn shows a card. Others in the group help to identify the word, and all the children say the word together. When all the words have been identified, go back to the first cards. On chart paper, write the words in a sentence (a silly one), using as few nonfocus connecting words as possible. Have the group read the sentence together, then continue in this way for the other words.
- **Cycle 2.** On a chart, write sentences using all the words from the children's word packs at least once. Provide the group with chips or tokens, and have each student lay out his or her cards in a row. The group then reads two or three sentences from the chart. Each child tries to locate words from the sentences among her or his cards; when a match is discovered, the child calls out the word (the others check) and places a chip on the appropriate card. The process is repeated until all cards are covered (or if cards remain uncovered after all the sentences have been read, the children simply say the words aloud and cover the cards).
- **Cycle 3.** For this check-up activity, you'll need graph paper and colored markers. Each child is assigned a column on the graph. Children then, in turn, draw words from their word packs and say them. Each time a child correctly identifies a word, quickly color in a box in the appropriate column. The children enjoy watching their graph lines grow as they develop mastery of their word packs.

Words should be reviewed often to see if they're being retained. Any that have become strangers go back into a word pack for recycling.

Idea by: Jackie Miller, Brigham City, Utah.

PARENT LISTENERS

An easy way for parents to become more familiar with their child's classroom and curriculum is for them to become "parent listeners." All that's needed is a bit of free time and some willing ears.

Each parent listener can work with a small group of children, listening to them read (stories they've written, themes based on current studies, texts) and then reading to them (teacher- or parent-selected material, such as biographies, short stories, even riddles and jokes). It's a great way to get parents involved in their child's schoolwork, and to get children involved in reading.
Idea by: Becky Alchin, Forest Elementary School, Farmington Hills, Mich.

WORD WALK

Words aren't limited to what is printed in books and periodicals. There are words on billboards, street signs, buildings—almost everywhere. A class word walk can be the beginning of a valuable reading activity. (From *The Alphabet Connection: A Parent's and Teacher's Guide to Beginning Reading and Writing,* Shocken.)

Provide the children with pencils and paper and take them on a walk around the block. Have them write down any or all words they see (you may want to stipulate the kinds of words to look for, depending on the age group and the locale). Back in the classroom, invite children to use their words in some or all of the following ways:

—list the words that begin with the same letter or sound;

—find the longest word, find the shortest;

—write a story using as many of the words as you can;

—categorize the words (for example, those relating to animals, or food, or traffic, etc.);

—separate words into those that are familiar and those that are not;

—look up the meanings of any new words.

You might want to have children work together to look up new words and to help each other with pronunciations of unfamiliar words. Or have children exchange their word lists to extend the activity.

GEOBOARD WORD MATCH

Geoboards, those square boards with equal rows of protruding pegs or nails, have traditionally been used in math, but also make excellent reading-skills aids. They can help teach opposites, beginning blends, vowel sounds or any number of reading basics.

Press the geoboard against a similar-size sheet of paper. The pegs will leave imprints on the paper that you can punch through with a scissors or compass point. The paper will then slide over the pegs and lie flat on the board.

Before putting the paper in place, however, write below each hole a word you want children to work with. When the paper is fitted over the pegs, a child (or small groups of children) can stretch rubber bands between the two words that are synonyms, or antonyms, or that have the same vowel sounds, or that end with silent *e*, and so on.

By using rubber bands of different colors, you can emphasize the connections. And laminating the word sheets will assure their long-term use.
Idea by: Andrea Nolley, Hugh K. Cassell Elementary School, Waynesboro, Va.

PINHOLE PROJECTIONS

Those disappointing slides that come back from the camera store totally black can provide the basic materials for a unique teaching aid. Simply take a needle and poke tiny holes in each slide to form whatever you choose to emphasize: letters of the alphabet, short words, punctuation marks for the reading curriculum; fractions, simple equations for math; constellations for science. The possibilities are infinite.
Idea by: Sister M. Francesca, St. Theodore's School, Rochester, N.Y.

MUSICAL SQUARES

Musical Squares is a bit like musical chairs, only instead of chairs there is an "alphabet sidewalk," and rather than sitting on a chair, the object is letter recognition.

The materials you'll need to construct the game include: 6½ yards of 36-inch clear, heavy plastic (sold in rolls in department stores), a yard or two of Con-Tact paper, two rolls of colored tape, and construction paper.

Cut the plastic in half lengthwise, and lay the two strips end to end to make one long strip (13 yards long and 18 inches wide). Use the Con-Tact paper as tape to hold the strips together. Next lay pieces of colored tape across the width of the plastic at 18-inch intervals, so that you have a runner of 18-inch squares.

Make letters of the alphabet from construction paper and tape each letter under one of the plastic squares. The letters will show through but will be protected from the Musical Squares shufflers.

Your "alphabet sidewalk" is now ready for a round of Musical Squares. Any number can play. One child chooses a secret square (letter), whispers it to the teacher and then stands aside to observe. The players walk the letter runway as music plays (piano, a record, or the "Alphabet Song" sung a cappella). When the music stops, the observer announces the secret square letter. (If letters are still new to the children, the letter may also be written on the chalkboard to help players with identification.) Everyone looks to see who's standing on the secret square letter. The child who is, wins—and so picks the next secret square. If the musical interludes are brief, there's more action—and more letter-recognition practice.

When the game is over, roll up the runner and store it in a large wrapping paper tube. And if you remove the construction paper letters, the sidewalk runner is ready for any other materials—numerals, shapes, words—you'd like to reinforce through Musical Squares.
Idea by: Linda Oggenfuss, Maywood, N.J.

WHAT'S IN A NAME?

Learning to identify vowels may be an easier task if students' names, rather than unfamiliar words, are studied. (From *Reading Fun and Games*, Rhythms Productions.)

Ask each student to write her or his first name on a piece of paper and to circle the vowels in it. Meanwhile, write the vowels across the top of the chalkboard. Now ask each student, one at a time, to tell you the vowels that appear in his or her name, and write down the vowels in the appropriate columns. The columns will become, in effect, a bar graph. When all the students have been called on, ask, "Which vowels are the most common in our class?" "Which are the least common?" You may wish to repeat the activity using last names.

STORYBOOK GARAGE SALE

Here's an unusual alternative to the standard book report that will set young minds turning. Instead of asking the traditional questions about people, places and events in stories students have read, ask each student to choose one character from a story and to consider what object that character might sell at a garage sale. Encourage students to give careful thought to what the item could be—something that represents or tells about the character. Once students have made their decisions, have them draw, make or bring in from home the chosen item. Set up a display of the wares and discuss why the items were chosen. Were students able to guess any characters by the items?
Idea by: Beverly Hershey, Lancaster, Pa.

Rx for Your Kids: 28 Great Games to Improve Reading Comprehension*

by Nicholas Criscuolo

To become truly competent readers, children must understand and retain what they absorb from the printed page. Though single words do convey meaning, teachers often put too much emphasis on phonics and the pronunciation of isolated words—all at the expense of better comprehension. Here are 28 classroom-tested activites that can help you improve your students' reading comprehension. And the doctor assures us—they won't hurt a bit!

Emotional outlet.   Ask each student to choose a main character from a story and write a list of feelings or emotions expressed by that character. All items on the list must start with the beginning initial of the character's first name. When the kids have finished their lists, have them share their choices with classmates, describing the circumstances in the story that led them to select those words.

Hold up the card.   Give each child a set of cards on which you've printed the names of the central characters in a particular story—one character per card. Then read some descriptive sentences about these characters and their functions in the story. Students are to identify the character being described and hold up the appropriately labeled card.

Quiz bowl.   Divide your class into small groups and have each present a quiz program based on several different stories found in the reading text. The stories should be divided into categories, such as travel, sports, nature, and so on. The groups may use additional sources of information—almanacs, encyclopedias, and travel brochures—to form questions dealing with designated categories. Then the groups can take turns presenting their quiz programs, with the rest of the class acting as contestants.

Fishbowl fun.   Have your kids write questions about stories they've read on small slips of paper, making sure to include the title of the story and the author's name. Fasten a paper clip to each slip and place them together in a fishbowl. Then make a "fishing pole" from a pencil, string, and small magnet. Let the kids "fish" for questions and attempt to answer them orally.

Story notebooks.   Ask each child to keep a small notebook entitled, "Stories I Have Read." After they've read a new story, have them answer the following questions in their notebooks:
    a. What is the name of the story?
    b. Who wrote it?
    c. Who are the main characters?
    d. Which character did you like best and why?
    e. What part of the story did you like best? Why did you like this part?
You might also want the kids to illustrate a major scene from each story on the pages opposite their answers.

Secret identities.   Have each child write a description of a famous character from literature—making sure not to divulge that character's name. For example:

I am brown and furry.
I love honey.
Christopher Robin is my best friend.
Who am I? (Winnie the Pooh)

The kids should take turns reading their descriptions aloud while the rest of the class tries to guess the characters' identities.

Story rolls.   Have your children choose their favorite stories and list the main events in sequence. Then let them illustrate the incidents, in order, on long sheets of butcher paper. When the drawings are finished, give each student two cardboard tubes (paper towel or aluminum foil rolls work best) and have each roll his or her illustrations from the first tube to the second and narrate the story for the rest of the class.

How would you feel?   You can help your kids recognize tone and feeling with this exercise that's unrelated to any particular story. Start by listing the following questions on your chalkboard under the heading, *Would you feel sad or glad if:*
   a. You could solve a mystery?
   b. Your bicycle was stolen?
   c. Your kite blew away?

Discuss these questions and the feelings they provoke with your class and continue the exercise by changing the initial adjectives to playful, serious, calm, nervous, and so on.

True or false?   Start by preparing several statements about a particular story, some true and some false. Then give each student two cards—one labeled "true" and the other labeled "false." As you read each statement aloud, instruct the children to hold up the appropriate card.

Mix-up.   Print the major events of a story on oaktag strips and place the strips in improper order on your chalkledge. Ask students to put the strips in their correct order, according to the sequence of events in the story. Repeat the procedure for several different stories.

Rewrites.   Have kids choose the final paragraph of a story they've recently read and use it as the starting point for original stories of their own. Or, you might want them to rewrite the last few paragraphs of a favorite story to give it a different ending. Then have the kids share their versions with classmates, asking them to supply new titles for the rewritten stories.

Paragraph pickings.   Divide the class into groups of two and let each pair choose a few paragraphs from a story with a lot of dialogue. They should practice reading the passage orally; then record their reading on cassette tapes. Make sure each pair tapes a summary of the events leading up to that paragraph first. Keep the tapes available for classmates to listen to in leisure time.

Recall sessions.   Divide the class into small groups and assign each group a different story to read. When everyone has finished reading, ask the kids to position themselves in a circle for this comprehension exercise. Lead off by stating the first main event in the story, then ask the student on your left to state the next, and so on around the circle.

Fortune cookie forecasts.   Have your kids make "fortune cookies" from folded brown construction paper. Now instruct the children to choose books or stories they've recently read and select one main character to focus on for this activity. Based on the actual events of the story, they are to make a prediction that might apply to the chosen character. Let each child put his or her prediction inside a fortune cookie and tape it shut. Place them all together in a large jar. Students are to take turns picking fortune cookies from the jar and guessing which character and story the prediction refers to. As a follow-up activity, you might also want the kids to write new endings to the stories, based on the predictions they've chosen.

Why did it happen?   Print the following sentences on your chalkboard and ask your kids to suggest possible reasons for each event. This exercise will help students improve their ability to make inferences and draw conclusions.
   a. It was a foggy day and the bird flew into the building.
   b. Mark brought a bowl of hot chicken soup over to his friends's house.

Rate it.   Encourage students to react critically to the stories they read through a numerical rating system. With your guidance, let the kids establish their own criteria for rating stories from poor to excellent. Then instruct them to make a chart for each story they read, listing the date, title, main characters, main idea, and the numerical rating.

Taping sessions.   Cut out several short stories from discarded basal readers, staple them together, and give one to each child in your class. Ask the kids to read and summarize their stories; then let them record these summaries on cassette tapes along with three comprehension questions that they make up. (Answers to these questions should be printed on an answer key.) Invite students to listen to their classmates' tapes, answer the comprehension questions, and then check their responses against the answer key.

Scrambled sentences. Help kids reinforce math and sequence skills with this exercise. Start by writing the following sentences on your chalkboard:

Anita handed the salesperson $9.
Anita decided to buy a pair of shoes.
Anita went to the large store's shoe department.
The salesperson said the shoes cost $7.
Anita selected a pair of black shoes.

Have the children number these sentences in their proper order, rewrite them in paragraph or math problem form, and compose a comprehension question to accompany it. In this case, the most logical question would be: How much change did Anita receive?

Act it out. Isolate particular episodes or events from several stories your class has recently read. Describe these events on small slips of paper and put them together in a jar. The kids should take turns drawing from the jar and acting out, charade-style, the events they pick. The rest of the class must guess which episode is being acted out and which story it took place in.

Swap shop. Ask the children to write descriptive paragraphs about a character or an event appearing in their reading text. Then divide the class into pairs and have the kids read their paragraphs aloud to their partners. The listener must identify the character described and give the name of the story he or she appeared in.

People predictions. Ask each child to choose a recently read story from the reading text, and to write a sentence predicting a future event in the life of one of its main characters. One by one, have the kids identify their characters for the rest of the class and attempt to convey their predictions, using gestures only.

Problem solving for fun. Choose student volunteers to form a panel to discuss the problems that major characters in recently read books or stories encounter. Try these questions for starters:

a. What major problem did the main character or characters face?
b. How was this problem solved?
c. Would you have done something different to solve the problem?

Key words. Have kids underline the important words in a story paragraph. They should then list these words in order of appearance and orally reconstruct the paragraph for classmates.

Marvelous mobiles. Have your kids make decorative hanging mobiles to illustrate major events in stories from their reading texts. They will need wire coat hangers, string, scissors, crayons, and paste. Have them begin by writing the titles and authors of the stories they've chosen on long strips of tagboard. Now each child should punch one hole at the top of this strip and fasten it with string to the bottom of the hanger. Next, have the kids punch several holes along the bottom of the title strip. From these holes, the kids should hang pictures from magazines and newspapers or original drawings that illustrate major events. These pictures should be mounted on construction paper and hung from the title strips in sequential order. The last hanging piece should be labelled with the student's name.

What happened next? Write the following statements on your chalkboard:

a. Sarah was riding very fast on her bike. She did not see the hole in the road. What happened next?
b. Chuck came home from school early. His head felt hot and his throat hurt. What happened next?

Ask children to explain what they think happened next, making sure they can defend their answers.

Story line. Draw a large grid on your chalkboard with the headings, *Scene, Characters, Location,* and *Action.* Choose a few stories your kids have recently read and ask for volunteers to fill in the outline you've drawn. This will reinforce your students' sequence skills and ability to summarize events.

Favorite scenes. Have kids construct scenes from their favorite books or short stories using papier mâché, bits of fabric, colored construction paper, string, or any other materials that would visually enhance the construction. Then let each child share his or her creation with the rest of the class, making sure to describe the events that led up to and followed the chosen scene.

Classified information. Have the children select particular situations from stories in their reading texts and use them as starting points for written classified ads. For instance, a story about a man who moves from Alaska to Florida could be the start of an advertisement selling a used snow blower.

A Potpourri of Game-Making Ideas for the Reading Teacher

by Sandra McCormick and
Betty M. Collins

In an era of informal education and individualization, many teachers are choosing to create their own educational materials rather than to purchase commercially prepared products. Unlike many commercial products, teacher-made activities and games can be designed to fit specific objectives for individual children. They add interest to the day's routine and often motivate students in ways that more conventional materials do not. Materials that are challenging and require individual involvement can capture and hold the attention of young learners more readily than worksheets, drills, or assignments such as "work all the exercises at the end of the chapter."

This article will help teachers who wish to create their own reading materials. Since many booklets are readily available describing learning materials teachers can make, no attempt is made here to provide instructions for the preparation of specific games or activities. Instead general hints and resources that can be used in preparation of various games and activities are offered. Your game/activity-making can be made easier and more successful by using the suggestions below.

MATERIALS, SOURCES, USES

- Blank playing cards are useful for dozens of purposes. These colorful cards resemble regular playing cards. They are coated with plastic, which adds to their durability in the classroom. The fronts of the cards are blank, so you can paste pictures on them, or write words or word parts, or write anything you wish your students to learn through a game. It is more fun to play a learning game based on rummy, Old Maid, or even poker when the cards used resemble the real thing.

One source from which blank playing cards can be purchased is: Sovereign Playing Card and Novelty Corporation, 200 Verdi Street, Farmingdale, New York 11735. In 1980 a box of 500 cards cost US $3.75 postpaid.

- Writing words or letters on blank playing cards can be a problem because of the plastic coating. Pencil does not show well, ballpoint pen doesn't work at all, and most felt tip marking pens smear. There are, however, certain types of pens that can be used. Pens designed for writing on overhead transparencies work well on the plastic coated cards; be sure to get the kind with permanent ink (not washable). The Staedtler Lumocolor pen is available in 12 colors at US $.80 each from Cherrys—H. Cole Co., 59 E. Spring Street, Columbus, Ohio 43215. Another usable pen is the Micropoint Super Marker, which marks on everything. These pens (US $.79) may be found where marking pens are sold.

You can also type the words onto the cards and coat the surface with clear fingernail polish to prevent the typewriter ink from smearing.

- Many children enjoy board games that allow them to move a marker along squares toward a goal. These games are useful for such things as increasing sight word recognition or practicing initial consonant sounds. Drawing many little squares, however, and getting them to look reasonably neat is a tedious chore. A good solution is to use a commercial gameboard to make a pattern. To do this, cover the commercial gameboard with a piece of tissue paper, using masking tape to secure it. Trace the pattern of squares with a pencil. Remove the tissue paper and attach it to the piece of posterboard or tagboard you plan to use for your game. With a felt tip pen trace the pattern you have previously drawn. The marks from the felt tip pen will soak through the tissue paper onto the posterboard producing a neat pattern with minimum effort. This works with both washable and permanent ink pens.

An opaque projector can also be used to project the pattern from a small commercial gameboard onto a piece of posterboard attached to a wall. The squares can then be outlined with a felt tip pen.

Posterboard to be used for games may be purchased in various colors in art supply, discount, department, or teacher stores. One sheet 22×28 inches (55×70 cm) costs approximately US $.29 to US $.45.

- Poker chips make good markers, or game pieces, to use with gameboards. The variety in the color of poker chips allows players to recognize their own markers quickly. Smaller poker chips are often available in adult game stores in sets of 100, with 20 chips in each of five colors. The smaller chips work well on the small spaces found on students' gameboards. You can also use buttons, coins, seashells, or small toys as markers.
- For other types of game pieces and a variety of items useful for game-making, a good source is: Marie's Educational Materials, Inc., P.O. Box 60694, Sunnydale, California 94088. At the time this article was written the following game pieces were available at these prices:

    Games markers—800 perforated paper markers to use with bingo and other games—US $1.00

    Spinners—20 of the two inch (5 cm) size—US $1.00

    Spinners—12 of the four inch (10 cm) size—US $1.50

    Blank lotto boards—Each board is 5 spaces by 5 spaces and 8×10 inches (20×25 cm) in size—US $.98

    File folder activities—10 gameboards that can be used with any reading series—US $5.95

- You may wish to decorate gameboards to suggest themes such as space, cars, sports, or cartoon characters. If you lack artistic ability, there are several alternatives. You can buy books of gummed stickers with pictures that appeal to children in art supply stores or stores that carry educational materials. One publisher of books of educational stickers is: Word Making Productions, Inc., Dept C., P.O. Box 15038, Salt Lake City, Utah 84115.

    Magazines such as *Sports Illustrated* or comic books are also good sources for pictures. Another technique is to use an opaque projector to project pictures onto a gameboard which has been attached temporarily to a wall. You simply draw around the projected image of the picture.

- Perhaps you'd like the gameboard itself to have the shape of something that interests your students, such as Snoopy, a race car, or an interstellar rocket. Again use the opaque projector to project a large image of the picture you want onto a piece of posterboard. Trace only the outline and cut it out. Instead of the usual rectangular gameboard, you now have one with the shape of a puppy, elephant, rabbit or truck.

- After constructing gameboards or other learning materials, you may wish to make them more durable by covering the posterboard with clear plastic. Clear plastic backed with adhesive is available in many discount stores and stores which sell wall coverings. It is sold under brand names such as Contac and Kwik Kover and usually ranges from US $.50 to US $.75 per yard or from US $2.00 to US $2.75 for a four yard (3.6 m) roll. It is generally 18 inches (45 cm) wide.

    There is a special trick to applying this plastic to posterboard. To avoid wrinkling or bubbling, cut a piece of plastic that is slightly larger than the piece of material you plan to cover. Remove the protective backing and place the plastic on a table with the adhesive side facing *up*. Then, lay the posterboard face down *onto* the plastic. You will find this method much neater than if you attempted to place the plastic onto the posterboard.

- For games or activities that require very sturdy material, pizza circles serve well. Pizza circles are the round pieces of cardboard on which pizzas are placed before being put into boxes at the pizza parlor. Their shape is suitable for many types of activities planned for individual work. One popular use is to divide the board into triangular shapes with a felt tip pen so that the board looks like a cut pie. Words, letters, syllables and so forth are written in each section. Students can match the information on each section of the board with information that has been written on clip clothespins. For example, lower case letters can be written on the sections of the pizza board and upper case letters printed on clothespins. The student clips upper case *H* to the section with the lower case *h,* and so forth. Many students enjoy activities such as this which involve manipulation. Most pizza shops will sell a few pizza circles to a teacher quite inexpensively.

● Teachers often spend time preparing independent activities that cannot be used again once students have marked their answers on them. Much time can be saved if the materials can be used more than once. To prepare permanent or semipermanent materials, write or draw reading activities on posterboard or oaktag. Instead of marking answers with a pencil, children can use poker chips, small sticks, or other removable markers to indicate their answers. Before the markers are removed, check students' responses and provide appropriate feedback. When the markers are removed, the material may be used again by other children having the same academic needs.

Another suggestion for preserving a thoughtfully prepared activity is to cover the material with clear adhesive plastic and direct the children to mark their responses with a crayon or washable felt tip pen. Answers may later be removed with a paper tissue dampened with water.

Some materials may also be prepared so that words, sentences and so forth can be used interchangeably. The same activity may be used by children working at varying levels or needing different types of practice. For example, when constructing the popular gameboards on which students move markers along a series of squares toward a final goal, it is often practical to leave the squares blank. Packets of cards can then be prepared from which students select a card requiring an appropriate response before they are allowed to move along the blank squares. If you prepare a variety of packets of cards, the same gameboard can be used by students at different levels of achievement and with different needs.

● To be worthy of use, a learning activity or game must have certain minimal characteristics. (1) Although you will usually provide some directions to students before they engage in an activity, most activities should be prepared so that students can engage in the activity without further teacher direction. (2) The activity must provide for *academic* learning, and not merely keep the students busy. (3) The activity must be at the appropriate level—neither too easy, nor too difficult—so that students can *learn* from it. (4) Some opportunity must be provided for *feedback* so students do not practice incorrect responses. (5) In most cases the activity should teach, not test.

In addition, you should ask yourself the following questions. Is the skill, concept, etc., for which this activity provides practice *important* to student learning? Will the activity be appealing/interesting to children? Is it attractive/neat? If there is handwriting on the product, is it of the high quality that should serve as a model for children? If appropriate to this particular activity, is the product durable?

Here are some selected sources of directions for specific reading games and activities that you can prepare using the suggestions in this article.

Bag of Tricks: Instructional Activities and Games by Janet Blake, Susan Ryberg, and Joan Sebastian. US $4.95. Love Publishing Company, 6635 East Villanova Place, Denver, Colorado 80222, USA.

Teacher-Made Materials for Language Arts compiled by Charles Curatalo. US $4.00. Mr. Charles Curatalo, New York State Migrant Center, State University College of Arts and Science, Genesco, New York 14454, USA.

Classroom Reading Games Activities Kit by Jerry Mallett. US $14.95. Center for Applied Research in Education, Inc., P.O. Box 130, West Nyack, New York 10995, USA.

Reading Games, volume 1, revised 1974, Orange. US $4.00 + US $.60 postage and handling. Greater San Diego Reading Association, P.O. Box 1298, La Mesa, California 92041, USA.

This Will Turn You On by Candy Carter. ED 095 534. Hard copy, US $1.50 + postage. ERIC Document Reproduction Service, P.O. Box 190, Arlington, Virginia 22210, USA.

Resource List

PRINT AND NONPRINT MEDIA

All about Letters. Rev. ed. (No. 01135) Urbana, IL: National Council of Teachers of English, 1982. 64p.

The United States Postal Service has helped produce this booklet, which is useful as an aid in composition classes. Secondary students are motivated to read and write letters through activities which include testimonials from famous persons, history of the postal service, and "how-to" tips on writing letters.

Annotated Bibliography for Mystery. Paula K. Montgomery, comp. Rockville, MD: Montgomery County Public Schools, Division of Instructional Materials, 850 Hungerford Drive, Rockville, MD 20850, 1979. 51p.

Intended to supply ways to entice reluctant readers to read mysteries. Identifies mystery novels for grades K-8. "Selection based on good writing style and well-developed plots that require the characters to solve well-defined problems." Arranged alphabetically by author, entries contain full bibliographic information, interest and readability level, and a one- or two-sentence annotation. Single copies are free.

Bantam's Young Adult Hotline. Bantam Books, School and College Sales Department, 666 Fifth Avenue, New York, NY 10103.

The hotline has been operating with success for the past few years and enables young adults to talk via a telephone hookup system to their favorite young adult authors. Schools must install the telephone system at their own expense.

Bauer, Caroline Feller. *This Way to Books*. New York: H.W. Wilson, 1982. 376p.

A collection of ideas, programs, techniques, and activities designed to involve children in books and to extend their reading experiences. Divided into seven major sections, each representing a method or theme for bringing children and books together.

Blostein, Fay. *Invitations, Celebrations*. Toronto, ON: Ontario Library Association, 1980. 233p.

Offers numerous ideas for getting students involved with books. Along with strategies for reaching reluctant readers and "celebrations" of the joy of reading are 700 annotations of the best of recent adolescent fiction.

"Books for the Teen Age." New York Public Library, 5th Avenue and 42nd Street, New York, NY 10018.

The pamphlet has 350 new works among its 1,250 entries which are arranged by subject and include film, photography and video, poetry, dance, music, women, love, sex, and drugs. A list called "Easy-to-Read Books for Teenager—1981" is also available and includes 70 works of fiction and 120 of nonfiction, some on a grade 1–4 reading level.

Children's Book Council, 67 Irving Place, New York, NY 10003.

The council supplies posters, bookmarks, reading lists, and bibliographies on a variety of topics. Upon request, the council will also supply a catalog of its holdings.

Ciani, Alfred J., ed. *Motivating Reluctant Readers*. (No. 530) Newark, DE: International Reading Association, 1981. 112p.

Nine articles, written by different authors, present a wide variety of suggestions for creating reading interest, both in the school and at home. Suggests a variety of ways to create a desire for reading, especially with reluctant youngsters.

Forgan, Harry. *Read All About It*. Santa Monica, CA: Goodyear, 1979. 182p.

The author has targeted 13 interest areas that kids always find fascinating—such as Magic Tricks, Spotlight on Sports, Jokes and Riddles, and Animals—and turned them into reading activities. For each interest area, there are 12 activities plus a list of books for further reading and information on free materials to send away for.

Gaskins, Irene W. "A writing program for poor readers and writers and the rest of the class, too." *Language Arts* 59 (November-December 1982): 854–61.

Using writing to motivate students to read has been effective with both good and poor readers. This article introduces a new approach to writing, explains organization of the classroom and the program, and describes a three-step procedure to teach writing, using a process approach.

Gentile, Lance M. *Using Sports and Physical Education to Strengthen Reading Skills.* Newark, DE: International Reading Association, 1980. 91p.

Written primarily for coaches and physical education instructors, this booklet may also be used by reading teachers to diversify their programs and motivate students to read. The ideas and exercises presented are intended to combine the forces of intellectual and physical activity and have been developed through actual teaching. Appended is a bibliography for sports and physical education with grade-level of reading difficulty indicated. Books, magazines, paperback books, and other references are provided in such areas as baseball, basketball, football, gymnastics, tennis, track and field, volleyball, soccer, hockey, swimming, and horseback riding.

Glazer, Susan M. *How Can I Help My Child Build Positive Attitudes toward Reading?* (No. 879) Newark, DE: International Reading Association, 1980.

Suggests ways of developing routine activities to foster the love of language necessary for building positive feelings about reading. Other titles in the series include: *Why Read Aloud to Children?* (No. 877) by M.T. Chan; *How Can I Encourage My Primary-Grade Child to Read?* (No. 875) by Kayes Ransbury; *How Can I Help My Child Learn to Read English as a Second Language* (No. 874) by Marcia Baghban; *How Does My Child's Vision Affect His Reading?* (No. 873) by Donald W. Eberly; *How Can I Get My Teenager to Read?* by Rosemary Winebrenner; and three booklets by Norma Rogers: *How Can I Help My Child Get Ready to Read? What Books and Records Should I Get for My Preschooler?* and *What is Reading Readiness?* Booklets are available from the IRA.

Harris, Albert J., and Sipay, Edward R. *How to Teach Reading: A Competency-Based Program.* New York: Longman, 1979. 631p.

This book is a reference tool for teaching reading and includes 11 modules designed to organize the content for a college course. However, "Instilling the Desire to Read," (Unit 10) is of particular interest to the teacher and librarian concerned with a student's motivation to read.

Kusnetz, Len. *Your Child Can Be a Super Reader.* Roslyn Heights, NY: Learning House, 1980. 122p.

Written for parents, the book contains motivational activities for developing reading skills and reading enjoyment in children. Information is available on understanding reading test scores, organizing a vocabulary-building program, monitoring children's reading progress, choosing books and magazines, obtaining free materials, etc.

Lawrence, Paula. *Ready, Set, Read!* Lincoln, NE: GPN, 1980.

This reading comprehension program for children, produced by the Tucson Public Library, contains a 38-page manual and two videotapes centered around activities to encourage reading comprehension and promote word recognition. The materials may be ordered from the Great Plains National Instructional Television Library, PO Box 80669, Lincoln, NE 68501.

Mason, George E., and Blanchard, Jay S. *Computer Applications in Reading.* Newark, DE: International Reading Association, 1979.

Examines the use of computers in the teaching of reading and their past, present, and future potentials.

Miller, Mary Susan. *Bring Learning Home.* New York: Harper and Row, 1981. 256p.

Home is a vital part of the schooling process. This book offers advice on motivation, how children can get along with teachers, the home role in learning, parent-child communication, discipline, school problems, and educational programs.

Monson, Dianne L., and McClenathan, DayAnn K., eds. *Developing Active Readers: Ideas for Parents, Teachers, and Librarians.* Newark, DE: International Reading Association, 1979. 104p.

Contains 11 articles giving suggestions for interesting activities to involve children in reading. Divided into parts, the first section gives ideas for selecting books and introducing children to libraries; the second recommends ways to help children respond to literature and interact more completely with books.

''New Channels to Reading.'' San Diego, CA: Department of Education/San Diego County, 1979.

The program is an attempt to find a student-centered way of teaching literacy skills to secondary students. It uses student interest in television and in films as the channel through which to learn and to use reading and writing skills in the study of quality literature. For information on the program write: Katharine A. Kane, Project Manager, 6401 Linda Vista Road, San Diego, CA 92111.

News for Parents from IRA. Newark, DE: International Reading Association.

The purpose of this two-page, triannual newsletter, which is produced three times a year, is to provide practical tips for parents to help their children learn to read and want to read. The educator will find these suggestions useful in the classroom; the newsletter can be duplicated and sent home with students.

Posters and Bookmarks. American Library Association, Public Information Office, 50 East Huron Street, Chicago, IL 60611.

Materials for stimulating reading interest in the library or classroom—promotional posters, bookmarks, brochures, and pamphlets—are available from the American Library Association. A current catalog is available upon request.

Reading for Fun: How to Establish a Motivational Reading Program for Children. Lawrence, KS: University of Kansas, n.d. 26p.

The pamphlet gives a brief history of the University of Kansas's Children's Reading Program and then relates the why, where, and how of starting such a program. Considers a number of typical initial problems in establishing a motivational reading program. Contains helpful sections on materials, financing, sponsors, record keeping, and motivational ideas.

"The Reading Program and the School Media Center." Chicago: American Association of School Librarians/American Library Association, 1976.

Lists books and articles useful for reference; provides instruction on how books should be correlated between the school reading program and media center.

"Reading with Children Through Age 5." Child Study Children's Book Committee at Bank Street College, 610 West 112th Street, New York, NY 10025.

Lists more than 250 titles and is arranged into categories such as: "About Children," "People and Families," and "Humor and Folk Tales." Entries are grouped by age and interest and include brief annotations.

Robbins, John. *Readit*. Bloomington, IN: Agency for Instructional Television, 1982.

Supplies 16 15-minute videocassette programs (with teacher's guide) designed especially for students in grades three through five. Programs cover adventures, fantasies, histories, and biographies and feature narration of portions of the texts, narrator illustrations at an easel, animated segments, and cliff-hanging endings to motivate students to seek out the books in the library. Programs may be rented or purchased from the agency. Preview cassettes which give an overview of the programs are available.

Smith, Carl B., and Elliot, Peggy G. *Reading Activities for Middle and Secondary Schools*. New York: Holt, Rinehart and Winston, 1979.

Provides the secondary school teacher with "how-to-do-it" suggestions in specific subject areas in order to teach reading. The book is arranged according to types of reading problems, allowing teachers to identify activities throughout the book for specific problem areas.

Spiegel, Dixie Lee. *Reading for Pleasure: Guidelines*. Newark, DE: International Reading Association, 1981. 89p.

Both theory and practice involved in developing reading for pleasure are included. The importance of recreational reading as an adjunct to the regular program is supported by research reviewed in the theoretical portion of the book. The practical aspects of a recreational reading program are then discussed. These include: motivating the students to participate, initiating the program, and managing the time and materials.

"25 Ways Parents Can Help With Reading." Department of Elementary and Secondary Education, PO Box 480, Jefferson City, MO 65102. 1979.

Included in the brochure are ideas that parents can use to help their children to read, as well as information on reading skills. A copy is available free from the above address.

Weiner, Elizabeth Hirzler, ed. *Unfinished Stories for Facilitating Decision Making in the Elementary Classroom*. Washington, DC: National Education Association, 1980. 78p.

Contains story beginnings to be completed through discussions and/or writing to motivate students to think critically. Topics in this book include responsibility and commitment to oneself and others, personal shortcomings, and shortcomings of others. These activities could be used effectively as springboards to further reading.

White, Mary Lou, ed. *Adventuring with Books: A Booklist for Pre-K–Grade 6*. 1981 ed. Urbana, IL: National Council of Teachers of English, 1981. 472p.

Features approximately 2,500 new children's titles selected by the 15-member NCTE Elementary Booklist Committee. Books listed are recommended for their literary merit, high potential interest for children, and equitable treatment of minorities. Annotations summarize the stories and note age levels, bibliographical information, and awards.

DOCUMENTS AND REPORTS*

Ball, Diane A. *RIF + USSR = R.E.A.D*. Teaching Guide (052); Evaluative Report (142), 1981. 6p. (ED 195 944; EDRS.)

A junior high school reading program, Reading for Enjoyment and Development (READ), that combines the Reading is Fundamental (RIF) inexpensive book distribution program and the practice of entire school participation in uninterrupted sustained silent reading (USSR) is described. The development of the project and practical aspects such as scheduling, picking up the books wholesale, and promoting staff support are given.

Cassidy, Jack. *Selected Reading Language Arts Activities for Gifted and Able Junior High School Students*. Harrisburg, PA: Pennsylvania State Department of Education, Bureau of Curriculum Services, 1980. 17p. (ED 196 201; EDRS.)

The author describes some of the techniques used in the Pennsylvania Comprehensive Reading Arts Plan, which provides reading/language arts activities for junior high school-level gifted students. It is explained that the plan experiences include responding to literature, sustained silent reading of self-selected books, oral and written composition, and investigating and mastering language patterns.

---

*The entries in this section were taken from a search of the ERIC document files. Some of the annotations have been edited or abbreviated.

Catt, Martha E., ed. and others. *"The Funnybone Club" 1980. A Librarian's Planning Handbook.* Indianapolis, IN: Indiana State Library, 1980. 22p. (ED 203 875; EDRS.)

This guidebook contains suggestions for librarians interested in developing programs which will stimulate children's reading interests and improve their reading skills. Chapters describe program planning, record keeping, storytelling, and children's games. A bibliography of 18 sources of possible program activities and a graded list of humorous books for children are provided.

Ciccone, F. Dawn. *Reading Attitudes and Interests of Sixth Grade Pupils.* Master's thesis, Kean College of New Jersey, April 1981. 40p. (ED 200 928; EDRS.)

A study was conducted to discover if the stated reading attitudes and interests of sixth-grade students were relevant to their self-selected reading materials. Fifty students completed questionnaires concerning their reading attitudes and interests and used log sheets to record information about their self-selected reading materials. The majority of the students reported that they preferred to choose their own reading materials as opposed to having someone else select them. The findings indicate that student reading attitudes and interests are relevant to self-selected reading materials.

"Elaborating the Reading Curriculum for the Gifted." Cornette, James and others. May 1981. 28p. Paper presented at the Annual Meeting of the International Reading Association, April 27–May 1, 1981, New Orleans, LA. (ED 207 016; EDRS.)

Intended for reading teachers with gifted students, this paper outlines the characteristics of a gifted reader and suggests methods for adapting the reading curriculum to the needs of such students.

Epstein, Ira. *Measuring Attitudes Toward Reading.* ERIC/TM Report 73. Princeton, NJ: ERIC Clearinghouse on Tests, Measurement, and Evaluation, November 1980. 145p. (ED 196 938; EDRS.)

A reading program's effectiveness can be assessed by investigating skills improvement together with attitude improvement. Frequently, teachers make questionable assumptions about student reading attitudes. To provide educators with a more accurate picture of students' expressed feelings, students' attitudes toward reading should be measured with formal assessment techniques. After reviewing the nature of reading attitudes, various attitude measurement techniques are described, such as Likert scales, the Guttman cumulation technique, the semantic differential, interviews, and observation rating scales. A source book of 14 reading attitude instruments is appended.

"Incorporating Fun Activities within Mastery Learning Units." Mann, Sylvia B. and Fridell, Ronald. May 1980. 14p. Paper presented at the Annual Meeting of the International Reading Association, May 5–19, 1980, St. Louis, MO. (ED 188 122; EDRS.)

"Fun activities" such as games, puzzles, discussions, debates, drama, and art are used in every unit of the Chicago Mastery Learning Reading/Learning Strategies program. Activities include: (1) ungraded optional activities, (2) enrichment activities, and (3) subject-related applications.

"Individualizing a Middle School Reading Program." Bell, Louise C. May 1981. 9p. Paper presented at the Annual Meeting of the International Reading Association, April 27–May 1, 1981, New Orleans, LA. (ED 204 742; EDRS.)

The individualized reading approach is a means of teaching reading to middle school students using self-selection of books by students, individual teacher-student conferences, and grouping according to needs and interests. Before selecting books for the program, a teacher should survey students to determine their reading attitudes and interests. The classroom should provide a place for individual conferences, ease of movement, and possibly a learning center offering skill enhancement activities. Activities which provide opportunities for students to share what they have read include writing an advertisement for the book, writing a television program based on the story, and designing a book jacket.

A Parent's Guide to Reading Instruction. Harrisburg, PA: Pennsylvania State Department of Education, Bureau of Curriculum Services, 1981. 29p. (ED 201 998; EDRS.)

The 12 articles in this publication contain information designed to help parents of preschool and elementary school children understand the complex psychological and sociological process of language development and its relationship to learning how to read. The articles also provide specific suggestions for parents who wish to participate in their child's reading development.

"Promising Practices for Improving Reading Attitudes." Turner, Thomas N., and Alexander, J. Estill. February 1980. 25p. Paper presented at the Annual Meeting of the Southeastern Regional Conference of the International Reading Association, February 6–9, 1980, Nashville, TN. (ED 188 108; EDRS.)

The research on the effect of attitudes on reading is reviewed in this paper to support the position that the affective part of learning is as important to learning to read as well as the cognitive part. Suggestions for improving reading attitudes are given. Activities are suggested for five forms of creative reading: (1) model imitations; (2) idea extension, elaboration, and augmentation; (3) visualization, (4) incorporation, and (5) contradictory or supporting reading. On the premise that effective work with questions can help reading attitudes, 18 ideas for questioning games are described.

Schrenker, Cecilia, ed. "Evaluating Reading Programs." *Wisconsin State Reading Association Journal* 25 (4) (May 1981). 40p. (ED 204 704; EDRS.)

The seven articles in this journal issue focus on the evaluation of reading programs at the elementary and secondary levels. The articles contain: (1) guidelines for evaluating reading materials; (2) a checklist designed to provide a broad overview of a school reading program; (3) an interview with well-known author and educator Wayne Otto concerning techniques for evaluating reading programs; (4) a list of publications designed to keep parents informed about reading instruction; (5) a criticism of programs designed to prepare all children to read at the same grade level; (6) a list of questions to be asked by teachers when evaluating a classroom reading program; and (7) a rating scale evaluating secondary school reading programs.

See, Hear and Do: Building a Positive Attitude. Parent Participation—A Formula for Success. Indianapolis, IN: Indiana State Department of Public Instruction, Division of Reading Effectiveness, 1980. 31p. (ED 201 982; EDRS.)

This booklet focuses on developing a positive attitude toward reading. Divided into three sections, the booklet describes activities for parents to use with their children to motivate them to read. Suggested reading experiences are to relate television and reading, start a home library and reading center, encourage oral reading, and present books as gifts.

Spiegel, Dixie Lee. *Reading for Pleasure: Guidelines*. ERIC Clearinghouse on Reading and Communication Skills and International Reading Association, 1981. 96p. (ED 204 722; International Reading Association, 800 Barksdale Road, PO Box 8139, Newark, DE 19711.)

Intended for classroom teachers and administrators who want their schools to reflect commitment to the idea that reading for pleasure is an essential part of every successful reading program. This book provides suggestions by which educators can coordinate their efforts with librarians and parents to get children to read voluntarily.

''These Worked—Try Them.'' Kochinski, Gerald J. May 1980. 15p. Paper presented at the Annual Meeting of the International Reading Association, May 5–9, 1980, St. Louis, MO. (ED 186 873; EDRS.)

The paper contains descriptions of activities that have proven successful in one middle school's reading program. Each description contains a commentary on the activity, its objective, the skills it reinforces or teaches, and the materials needed. Among the activities presented are a method of teaching vowel sounds, a creative writing activity involving cartoon strips, a technique for teaching syllabication, a means of criteria-reference testing on a low budget, and methods for implementing and maintaining a sustained silent reading program. The author also provides information about the school where the activities were developed and about its reading program and a discussion of sustained silent reading.

Whitfield, Eddie L. and Dickey, Wayne B. *Developing and Implementing an Individualized Reading Program*. 1980. (ED 191 011; EDRS.)

Effective individualized reading programs can mean the difference between success and failure for children with reading problems. There are five areas to be considered in the implementation of such a program: (1) diagnosis or needs assessment; (2) flexible grouping, based on achievement, special needs, interest, social background, or a peer tutoring relationship; (3) material selection; (4) a balance of teaching methods; and (5) a personalized reading approach that involves an abundance of books in the classroom, student/teacher conferences, and development of a student's incentive to improve his/her skills.

Index

Compiled by Linda Schexnaydre